Paula   Leebert

718- 282 - 1310

973-   201-894-5906

Carlton

Heidi Clarke

Pleasures Of The Palate

Pleasures Of The Palate

Harris Golden

GOLDEN'S KITCHEN

PHOENIX, ARIZONA

Designed by:

Harris Golden

Food Styling and Photography:

Harris Golden

Editing:

Candice Miles

Assistant Editing:

Pauline Yearwood and Elizabeth Teitel

Illustrating:

Sandy Golden

Typesetting:

Noreen Delmont

Graphic Art:

Jaci Young

Color Separating:

American Color

Printing:

O'Neil Printing

Heinz ketchup bottle in photograph is used by permission of the H.J. Heinz Company.

Page 62 is reprinted from the Prophet by Kahlil Gibran, by permission of Alfred A. Knopf, Inc. Copyright 1923 by Kahlil Gibran and renewed 1951 by Administrators C.T.A. of Kahlil Gibran Estate and Mary G. Gibran.

Library of Congress Catalog Number 88-081018

ISBN 0-9620669-0-7

Published by Golden's Kitchen
2811 East Calaveros Drive, Phoenix, Arizona 85028

Printed in the U.S.A.

To Erika,

the latest family addition,

just in time for this edition.

and

To the Maine Chance guests

for their constant support.

About The Author

HARRIS GOLDEN

Harris Golden is a food consultant and menu designer for the hospitality industry, and is also the author of *Golden's Kitchen: The Artistry of Cooking and Dining on the Light Side*.

Executive chef for fourteen years at the exclusive Elizabeth Arden's Maine Chance beauty resort in Phoenix, Arizona, he lectures on and demonstrates the artistry of cooking for an international clientele.

An advocate of healthful fine dining, Mr. Golden belongs to the Nutrition Today Society, American Culinary Federation, and Les Amis D'Escoffier Society. He holds an Associate of Art degree in culinary arts, and a Bachelor of Science degree in hotel administration.

Contents

Introduction

I love the action of the kitchen: quickly slicing colorful vegetables with a sharp, well-balanced French knife; hearing them crackle in a hot, heavy metal pan riveted to a handle lying snugly in the palm of my hand. With two quick snaps of the wrist, the vegetables are mixed and browned on all sides. The aroma is enticing. Food is entertainment. Cooking is the only art that appeals to each of our senses — sight, touch, taste, smell, and hearing.

Throughout the production of this book, I have tried to capture the sense of excitement food offers — its beauty, intimacy, and humor. Scattered among the recipes are quotations, stories about food, personal experiences, and other surprises that are yours to discover. The second half of the book contains photographs of every recipe placed together so that you can sit back and browse undisturbed by any recipe type. More than a compilation of tasty, healthful, and workable recipes, this book should be a source of culinary entertainment for many years to come.

With no further ado, I would like to thank you for your participation and present to you — *Pleasures Of The Palate.*

Of all the arts,

cooking is the most ephemeral.

Hours of arduous devotion yield a masterpiece

that vanishes through the portals of the kitchen

leaving only a memorable repast.

Recipe Symbols

The following are recipe symbols found throughout the book and their meanings:

EASY TO PREPARE
(less than 30 minutes preparation time)

MODERATELY EASY TO PREPARE
(from ½ hour to 1½ hours preparation time)

MODERATELY DIFFICULT TO PREPARE
(from 1½ hours to 2½ hours preparation time)

DIFFICULT TO PREPARE
(more than 2½ hours preparation time)

The chef symbols also take into consideration the degree of difficulty of the task performed.
They do not take into account baking, cooking, marinating, dough rising,
and other times when there is no actual work involved.

A SMALLER PORTION CAN SERVE AS AN EXCELLENT APPETIZER
BEFORE THE DINNER ENTRÉE

Freshness is the essence of good cuisine.

When preparing the recipes,

use fresh meat, fish, fowl, fruits,

vegetables, herbs, garlic, ginger...

whenever possible.

Hors D'Oeuvres

and

Beverages

Hors D'Oeuvres Janette

chicken, pepper, and cashew nut mixture rolled in red leaf lettuce, and stuffed in cherry tomatoes

(Makes approximately 40 hors d'oeuvres)

Ingredients:
4 cups finely diced cooked chicken
½ cup dried currants
¼ cup finely diced red bell pepper
¼ cup finely diced yellow bell pepper (substitute green pepper if not available)
¼ cup fresh cut chives
1 cup finely chopped cashew nuts
2 tablespoons minced ginger
½ cup Chinese rice vinegar
½ cup light sesame seed oil
½ teaspoon cayenne pepper
1 teaspoon salt
1 head red leaf lettuce or green leaf lettuce
1 pint cherry tomatoes
parsley sprigs
some small flowers

Method:

1. Mix together the chicken, currants, bell peppers, chives, nuts, ginger, vinegar, oil, cayenne pepper, and salt.

2. Wrap half of the mixture into red leaf lettuce leaves. Cut the tops off the cherry tomatoes, stuff with the remaining mixture, then replace the tops.

3. Alternate the hors d'oeuvres on a large serving platter. Garnish the platter with parsley and flowers.

Photograph on page 239

Zucchini and Green Bean Canapés

(Makes 2 dozen canapés)

Ingredients:
¾ pound fresh or frozen green beans
1 cup chicken stock or canned chicken consommé
1 piece whole wheat bread
2 teaspoons raisins
¼ teaspoon cumin
salt and black pepper, to taste
1 large zucchini, cut into ¼-inch round slices
2 purple onions

Method:

1. Cook the green beans in the chicken stock until they are soft and the stock has been reduced to a syrup. Pass the beans, bread, and raisins through a meat grinder or chop in a food processor. Add cumin, and season with salt and pepper.

2. Scoop or spoon out the mixture onto the zucchini rounds, and arrange the prepared canapés on a serving platter.

3. Garnish each canapé with a triangle cut from one of the purple onions, and garnish the center of the platter with a water lily onion (see illustration).

Photograph on page 203

cut perpendicular slices
and place in simmering
water for approximately
30 seconds until onion is
limp to form water lily.

Spinach Puffs

(Makes 2 dozen puffs)

Ingredients:
⅔ cup water

4 tablespoons butter or margarine

⅔ cup unbleached, all-purpose flour

3 large eggs

¼ cup chopped green onion

1 tablespoon butter or margarine

1½ cups milk

3 tablespoons unbleached, all-purpose flour

1 bay leaf

2 heads spinach, cleaned, chopped, blanched in boiling water for 10 seconds, then well drained

2 pieces well-cooked bacon, crumbled into pieces

salt and black pepper, to taste

decorative greens

Method:

1. Preheat oven to 400 degrees.

2. In a saucepan, bring the water to a boil with 4 tablespoons of butter. Pour ⅔ cup of flour into the boiling mixture. Cook the paste over low heat, beating it rapidly with a wooden spoon until the ingredients are thoroughly combined and the mixture cleanly leaves the sides of the pan to form a ball. Remove the pan from the heat, and let cool. Beat the eggs, one at a time, into the mixture.

3. Spoon, scoop, or bag out the mixture on a lightly oiled or nonstick baking pan. Bake for approximately 30 minutes until brown and crisp.

4. While the shells are baking, sauté the onion in the tablespoon of butter until it is soft and translucent. Add 1½ cups of milk, 3 tablespoons of flour, and the bay leaf. Cook and stir until the mixture comes to a boil and thickens. Remove the bay leaf, add the chopped spinach, crumbled bacon, salt, and pepper.

(Recipe continued on next page.)

5. Remove the top portion of the pastry shells. Stuff with the spinach mixture. Spinach puffs may be prepared well ahead of time to this point. They also freeze well.

6. Before serving, heat the puffs in a preheated, 400 degree oven for 10 minutes. Transfer puffs to a serving tray, and garnish with decorative greens.

Photograph on page 198

Cucumber and Crabmeat Canapés

(Makes 24 canapés)

Ingredients: 2 large cucumbers
¼ pound chopped, cooked crabmeat, preferably from Alaskan King crab
3 tablespoons mayonnaise
½ teaspoon lemon juice
1 tablespoon chopped parsley
½ teaspoon cayenne pepper
24 slices of canned pimiento
lemon flower basket (see illustration)

Method: 1. Using a channeling knife, score the cucumbers lengthwise, and cut them into 1-inch round pieces. Using a melon baller, scoop out most of the seeds from the center leaving some to form a cup.

2. Mix the crabmeat, mayonnaise, lemon juice, parsley, and cayenne pepper together. Distribute crabmeat mixture into the center of each cucumber cup, and garnish with a slice of pimiento.

3. Place the canapés on a serving platter, and garnish the center of the platter with a lemon flower basket (illustration on next page).

Photograph on page 212

Lemon Flower Basket

Method:

1. Cut off bottom of lemon so that it will rest on a flat surface.

2. Using a stripper knife, score around the "equator" of the lemon, and make decorative scores resembling basket weaving on the lower half of the lemon.

3. With a paring knife, make 2 slices from the top of the lemon down through the center to form the basket handles. Cut zigzag edges around the lemon leaving only the basket handles on the top half of the lemon. Remove lemon pulp between the basket handles.

4. Fill the basket with small flowers.

Photograph on page 212

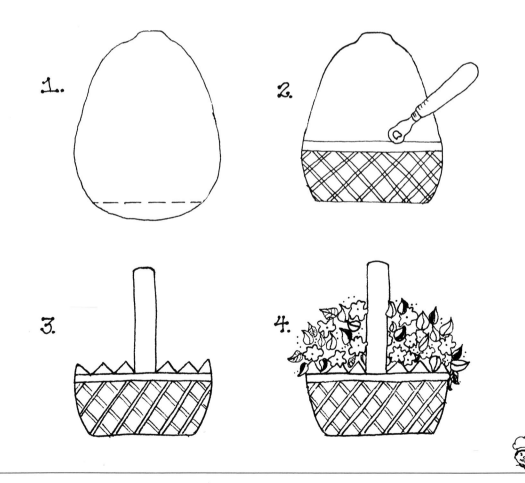

Orange Freeze

(Makes six 8-ounce servings)

Ingredients: 1 12-ounce can 100% concentrated, frozen orange juice, defrosted
24 ounces crushed ice
12 ounces club soda
strawberry ice cream (optional)

Method: 1.   Place the concentrated orange juice, ice, and club soda into a blender. Blend until a thick slush is formed. Pour into chilled serving glasses, and garnish with a small scoop of strawberry ice cream.

Photograph on page 191

Sparkling Rosé Punch

Everyone who enjoys entertaining should have a recipe for punch that is simple to prepare and works — that is, appeals to most people's taste buds. Here's one:

(Makes 2½ quarts punch)

Ingredients: 1 10-ounce package frozen strawberries
1 6-ounce can frozen lemonade
1 fifth rosé wine
1½ quarts 7Up
kiwi slices or lime slices

Method: 1.   Purée the strawberries, lemonade, and rosé wine in a blender. Just before serving, add the 7Up and kiwi or lime slices.

Photograph on page 171

Ricky Hors D'Oeuvres

black-eyed peas with jalapeno pepper, green onion, cilantro, and bell pepper on cucumber rounds

(Makes 3 dozen hors d'oeuvres)

Ingredients:
2 cups black-eyed peas
8 cups water
1 bay leaf
1½ teaspoons salt
¼ cup vegetable oil
2 jalapeno peppers, minced
1 cup chopped green onion
2 tablespoons chopped cilantro or parsley
3 cucumbers
red, green, and yellow bell peppers, cut into triangular strips
parsley sprigs

Method:
1. In a large, heavy metal pot, add the black-eyed peas, water, bay leaf, salt, and oil. Cook over medium flame for approximately 1 hour until the liquid has been totally reduced and absorbed by the peas.

2. Remove from heat. Remove bay leaf. Mash, and mix in jalapeno pepper, green onion, and cilantro.

3. Using a channeling knife, score the cucumbers lengthwise, and cut them into ½-inch rounds. Lay out cucumber rounds on a large serving platter. Using a #60 ice cream scoop, scoop out pea mixture onto each cucumber round, then garnish each hors d'oeuvre with 2 strips of bell pepper. Garnish the platter with parsley sprigs.

Photograph on page 234

Jennifer's Snow Ball Hors D'oeuvres.

(Makes 3 dozen hors d'oeuvres)

Ingredients: 1½ cups Ricotta cheese
6 tablespoons chopped pecans
6 tablespoons raisins
1¼ cups unsweetened, shredded coconut
penguin centerpiece (see illustration)
parsley sprigs and flowers

Method: 1.   Mix the Ricotta cheese, pecans, and raisins together. Using a #60 ice cream scoop, scoop out balls, and roll them in the coconut.

2.   Place balls in paper hors d'oeuvre cups that have been placed around a penguin centered on a round 14-inch serving platter. Garnish with parsley sprigs and flowers.

Photograph on page 208

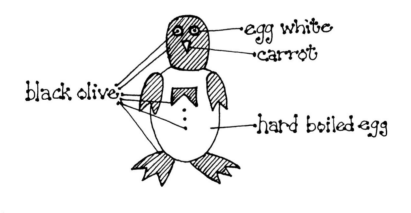

Belgium Endive and Salmon Salad Canapés

(Makes approximately 30 canapés)

Ingredients:
12 ounces cooked salmon

¼ cup mayonnaise or 2 tablespoons mayonnaise and 2 tablespoons 2% yogurt

1 tablespoon lime juice

1 teaspoon finely minced ginger

½ teaspoon salt

⅛ teaspoon cayenne pepper

4 or 5 heads Belgium endive

fresh chives

fresh dill weed

1 spider mum

Method:

1. Mix the first six ingredients together. Using a pastry bag with a plain piping tube, pipe out the salmon mixture onto the bottom of the Belgium endive leaves.

2. Garnish canapés with two 1-inch pieces of cut chives and a sprig of dill weed in the center. Place canapés on a large, round serving platter with the spider mum in the center.

Photograph on page 164

Carrot and Pea Hors D'Oeuvres

(Serves 6 to 8)

Ingredients:
1 8-ounce package Neufchatel cheese or cream cheese at room temperature
1½ tablespoons minced green chile peppers
1 clove garlic, minced
¼ teaspoon salt
⅛ teaspoon cayenne pepper
2 large carrots
1 small package frozen peas
fresh flower
parsley sprigs

Method:

1. Mix the cheese, chile peppers, garlic, salt, and cayenne pepper together until a smooth paste has formed.

2. Peel the carrots, and score them lengthwise with a channeling knife. Cut them into ½-inch-thick slices, and lay them out on a serving platter.

3. Using a pastry bag and a star tube, pipe out rosettes of cheese mixture onto each carrot. Top each rosette with a pea. Place the flower in the center of the platter, and garnish with parsley sprigs.

Photograph on page 162

Slow and steady is often the best way to win the race:

*   to make a good stew   *

*   to lose weight permanently   *

*   to achieve our aspirations   *

In this book is a turtle to remind us of this virtue.

Can you find the turtle?

Chicken Salad Erika

(Serves 6)

Ingredients:
2 cups finely diced, cooked chicken
¼ cup dried currants
2 tablespoons finely diced red pepper
2 tablespoons finely diced yellow pepper (substitute green pepper if not available)
2 tablespoons fresh cut chives
½ cup finely chopped cashew nuts
1 tablespoon ginger
¼ cup Chinese rice vinegar
¼ cup light sesame seed oil
¼ teaspoon cayenne pepper
½ teaspoon salt
3 tomatoes, halved
½ cup cooked Chinese snow peas
1½ cups cooked cauliflower buds
½ cup cooked black beans
1 pint radish sprouts
12 spinach leaves
12 Belgium endive lettuce leaves
6 Radicchio lettuce leaves
6 radish roses (make perpendicular cuts to form petals around the outside of the radish, then place in cold water to open petals)

Method:
1. Mix together the chicken, currants, bell peppers, chives, nuts, ginger, vinegar, oil, cayenne pepper, and salt. Scoop mixture out onto the tomato halves.

2. Mix the snow peas, cauliflower, and beans together.

3. Set up 6 plates according to the photograph, cover with plastic wrap, and refrigerate until serving.

4. Serve with your choice of dressing on the side (recipes on pages 42-44).

Photograph on page 174

Labor Day Salad with Lobster Dressing

This salad requires a bit of skill with a knife and cutting board.
Use a good knife with a very sharp blade.
Cut vegetables as uniformly as possible to achieve a polished-looking salad.
Refer to the illustration on the next page for cutting technique.
Good luck.

(Serves 6)

Ingredients:
1 bunch celery
1 red pepper
1 small can pitted black olives
1 small head red cabbage
1 head iceberg lettuce
1 head spinach
1 purple onion
8 radish roses (make perpendicular cuts to form petals around the outside of the radish, then place in cold water to open petals)
7 green onion curls (trim the green onions to 3 inches in length, then cut along the length of the green portion, leaving the bulb intact, and place in cold water to curl)

Method:

1. Cut the celery into ¼-inch-thick slices. Cut the red pepper into 1-inch diamonds. Mix the celery, red pepper, and olives together. Place the mixture lengthwise down the center of an oval platter.

2. Shred the cabbage, lettuce, spinach, and purple onion by slicing as thin as possible with a French knife. Place the red cabbage and lettuce in two separate mounds on one side of the celery mixture, and the spinach and purple onion in two separate mounds on the other side of the celery mixture.

3. Garnish the salad platter with the radish roses and green onion curls. Serve with Lobster Dressing on the side (recipe on next page).

Photograph on page 179

Lobster Dressing

(Makes 1 pint dressing)

Ingredients:
1   5-ounce frozen lobster tail
¼ cup dry white wine or dry vermouth
1 cup mayonnaise or ⅓ cup mayonnaise and ⅔ cup plain 2% yogurt
3 tablespoons tarragon vinegar
¼ teaspoon cayenne pepper
1 tablespoon chopped parsley

Method:

1.   Put the frozen lobster tail and the wine into a covered casserole that is suitable for microwave cooking. Cook on high for approximately 7 minutes. Let the lobster cool off, then deshell and chop the meat into fine pieces. Save the wine liquid from the casserole.

2.   Mix together the mayonnaise, vinegar, cayenne pepper, parsley, and wine liquid. Fold in the lobster. Refrigerate dressing until serving.

Photograph on page 179

chopping

slicing

My Worst Cut

"Did you ever cut yourself?" is a question most chefs hear even more often than "How long do you cook a twelve pound turkey?" (approximately 3½ hours in a 325 degree oven) or "Do you ever eat at McDonald's?" (only when I'm starving while traveling through a dilapidated town, or if my kids coerce me into the place).

Did I ever cut myself? Yes, and here for the record are the circumstances:

1.) I was attempting to cut frozen salami, a difficult task because of its concrete consistency and ability to roll all over a cutting board.

2.) The knife (I should say the weapon) hadn't been sharpened. As a result, all of my strength and weight was pressing heavily on a blade in an attempt to penetrate the surface of my frozen snack.

So the stage was set.

Warning:

The following may not be suitable for all readers.
If you wish to omit the sanguinary details, do not read between the parenthesis.

O.K. here it goes: (I'm not really going to describe the gore. Alfred Hitchcock believed it best to leave horrifying scenes to the imagination. My apologies to all ardent *Rambo* aficionados.)

Getting back to the story: The thumb of my left hand was moderately to severely severed — about a seven-and-a-half on a one-through-ten scale — and I could not stop the bleeding. Paper towels, gauze pads, direct pressure, elevation, and prayer were of no avail. At age fourteen, I was alone bleeding to death. So I called my mother at work and said those words that will turn a mother's hair white. "Mom, I cut myself and can't stop the bleeding."

My mother then managed an office for a caviar importing firm located in Manhattan's Greenwich Village. We lived in the northern part of Brooklyn: only twenty minutes away by car during normal traffic conditions; over an hour during rush-hour. Fortunately it was only 3:30 when I had come home from school looking for something to munch on.

My mother was on her way, and so was the fibrinogen in my wounded thumb. The blood was mostly staunched five minutes before my mother came frantically running through the door with a couple of people from her office — one to drive the car, and, I suppose, the other to keep her from passing out. I lived, and it was nice to have my mother home three hours earlier than usual. As for salami . . . I'll eat it if I'm starving to death while passing through a dilapidated town where there's no McDonald's.

Pryce Salad

breast of duck and vegetables basted with a soy and sesame seed dressing

(Serves 6)

Ingredients:
4 boneless duck breast halves, with the skin left on
1 cup julienne yellow straight-neck squash
1 cup julienne zucchini
1 cup julienne red bell peppers
1 cup julienne green bell peppers
¼ cup cut chives or green onion
6 cauliflower buds
6 broccoli spears
6 sprigs Mache lettuce or baby spinach or watercress
12 oyster mushrooms
6 bunches radish sprouts
6 Radicchio lettuce leaves
6 Boston lettuce leaves
Soy and Sesame Seed Dressing

Method:

1. Place the duck breasts, skin side down, in a large skillet. Cover the skillet, and cook over a low flame for approximately 7 minutes until the breasts have a slight trace of pinkness left in the center. Remove from the skillet, let cool awhile, then skin the breasts, and cut into julienne pieces.

2. In a pot of boiling water, blanch the squash, bell peppers, cauliflower, and broccoli, one at a time for a couple of minutes to soften the vegetables, but make sure that each one is still crunchy.

3. Arrange all the ingredients on 6 large salad or dinner plates according to the photograph. Cover the salad with plastic wrap, and hold in the refrigerator until serving time.

4. Just before serving, baste the salad — excluding the lettuce cups — with Soy and Sesame Seed Dressing (recipe on page 43).

Photograph on page 217

Three Bean Salad

(Serves 6)

Ingredients: 2 cups cooked black beans or pinto beans
2 cups cooked lima beans
2 cups cooked, cut green beans
⅓ cup olive oil
¼ cup red wine vinegar
¼ cup chopped purple onion
2 tablespoons chopped parsley
2 teaspoons chopped garlic
1 teaspoon chopped oregano
1 teaspoon granulated sugar
1 teaspoon salt
½ teaspoon black pepper
purple savoy lettuce or other decorative lettuce for underliners

Method: 1. Combine all ingredients excluding the lettuce, and refrigerate for a couple of hours to let beans marinate.

  2. Serve in a large bowl or individual salad plates lined with lettuce leaves.

Photograph on page 196

Purée of Fresh Pea Soup

(Serves 6)

Ingredients:
¼ cup chopped green onion or shallot
1 tablespoon butter or margarine
2 cups whole or 2% milk
2 cups strong chicken stock or canned chicken consommé
2 pounds fresh or frozen peas
salt and pepper, to taste
2 tablespoons finely julienned carrots
fresh marjoram leaves

Method:

1. In a large pot, sauté the onion in butter until translucent.

2. Add milk, stock, and peas. Cook uncovered until peas are just tender. Avoid overcooking the peas in order to maintain their bright color and fresh taste.

3. Purée the ingredients in a blender. Add milk or chicken stock to obtain the flavor and thickness desired.

4. Season with salt and pepper. Garnish with julienne carrot and marjoram leaves.

Photograph on page 178

Chilled Strawberry Soup

(Makes approximately 5 cups soup)

Ingredients: 2 pints strawberries
1 cup whole or 2% milk
½ cup plain 2% yogurt
1 tablespoon grated orange peel
juice of 2 medium oranges
⅛ teaspoon cinnamon
about 2 tablespoons granulated sugar
mint leaves

Method: 1.   Wash and stem strawberries. Reserve a few berries to garnish the soup.

2.   Purée the remaining berries, milk, yogurt, orange peel, orange juice, and cinnamon in a blender or a food processor.

3.   Sweeten the mixture to taste with sugar. The amount of sugar will depend on the natural sweetness of the strawberries and oranges.

4.   Distribute the soup into chilled bowls, and garnish each portion with a few thin slices of strawberries (cut from the reserved strawberries) and a few mint leaves.

Photograph on page 188

Gingered Chicken Breast Salad

(Serves 6)

Ingredients:
6 chicken breasts, skinned and boned
1½ cups strongly flavored chicken stock or canned chicken consommé
9 cups prepared tossed greens (a mix of spinach and green leaf lettuce in bite-sized pieces)
1 red bell pepper, cut into julienne pieces
¼ cup cashew nuts
¼ cup cut, fresh chives
fresh basil leaves
Belgium endive lettuce leaves
Sherry-Ginger Dressing

Method:

1. Poach the chicken breasts in simmering chicken stock. Refrigerate chicken breasts in the consommé until cool, then cut into julienne pieces.

2. Place 1½ cups of prepared tossed greens in the center of each of 6 large salad plates. Place the pieces of chicken in the center. Sprinkle with red pepper and cashew nuts. Garnish the top of the salad with a few basil leaves and the perimeter with Belgium endive lettuce leaves.

3. Cover with plastic wrap, and refrigerate until serving. Just before serving, baste each salad with Sherry-Ginger Dressing (recipe on page 44).

Photograph on page 218

Chrysanthemum and Onion Salad

(Serves 6)

Ingredients:　3 Spanish onions, thinly sliced
10 radishes, thinly sliced, and cut into half-moon pieces
cut chives
7 chrysanthemums
kale or other decorative lettuce leaves

Method:

1.　Blanch onions in boiling water for 30 seconds until slightly wilted but still crunchy. Set aside to cool.

2.　When the onions are cool, portion out on 6 salad plates, sprinkle with radishes, chives, and petals from one of the chrysanthemums.

3.　Garnish the plates with a chrysanthemum placed over a lettuce leaf.

4.　Serve with either Sherry-Ginger Dressing (recipe on page 44) or Soy and Sesame Seed Dressing (recipe on page 43).

Photograph on page 210

Marinated Cauliflower, Carrot, and Rutabaga Salad

(Serves 6)

Ingredients:
1 cup cauliflower buds
2 cups julienne carrots
2 cups julienne rutabaga
⅓ cup white wine vinegar
2 tablespoons olive oil
2 teaspoons granulated sugar
½ teaspoon salt
lettuce leaves
6 sprigs dill weed
6 red pepper medallions (see photograph)

Method:

1. Cook each vegetable separately until tender but still slightly crunchy.

2. In a large bowl, toss the vegetables with the vinegar, oil, sugar, and salt. Let marinate for at least 3 hours.

3. Portion out vegetables onto 6 plates lined with lettuce leaves. Garnish each plate with a sprig of dill and a red pepper medallion.

Photograph on page 214

Spinach, Beets, and Belgium Endive Salad

(Serves 6)

Ingredients: 2 heads Belgium endive
2 heads spinach, cleaned and separated into leaves
2 large, cooked beets, peeled and cut into julienne pieces
½ cup cut chives
1 hard-boiled egg, chopped
6 orchids or pansies

Method: 1. Place the endive leaves with stems facing the center on 6 salad plates. Lay out the spinach leaves with stems facing the center on top of the endive. Portion out beets and chives in the center of the salad, and sprinkle with chopped egg.

2. Garnish each salad with an orchid or pansy. Serve with your choice of dressing on the side (recipes on pages 42-44).

Photograph on page 176

Hearts and Flowers

(Serves 6)

Ingredients: 3 cups cooked green beans

24 hearts cut from red bell peppers with a heart hors d'oeuvre cutter

18 honeydew melon balls

18 rose petals

18 mint leaves

Raspberry-Walnut Dressing

Method:

1. Place ½ cup cooked green beans on each of 6 salad plates. Garnish each salad with 4 hearts, 3 melon balls placed inside 3 rose petals, and 3 mint leaves on the outside of the salad.

2. Serve Raspberry Walnut dressing on the side (recipe on page 44).

Photograph on page 230

Seafood Bisque

(Serves 6)

Ingredients: 2 pounds seafood in their shells (shrimp, crab, lobster in any combination) chopped into small pieces
2 cups chopped onions
2 tablespoons butter or margarine
6 tablespoons rice flour
1 teaspoon chopped garlic
6 cups whole milk
1 bay leaf
2 tablespoons sherry
¼ teaspoon cayenne pepper
2 tablespoons heavy cream (optional for extra richness)
salt, to taste
Garnish: cut pieces of truffle, cooked carrot, red bell pepper, radishes chives, red cabbage, zucchini, dill weed, and a cooked pearl onion

Method:

1. In a saucepan, cook the seafood and onions in the butter until there is a little browning. Add the rice flour and garlic. Stir, and cook for a minute. Stir in the milk and bay leaf. Cover the saucepan, and cook over a very low flame for approximately 1 hour.

2. Pass the mixture through a sieve or a food mill. Discard the contents left in the sieve or food mill including the over-cooked seafood and shells.

3. Add sherry, cayenne pepper, cream, and salt to the purée. Heat the bisque. Do not boil. Ladle into soup bowls, and garnish with the cut vegetables.

Photograph on page 193

Rossen Salad

(Serves 6)

Ingredients:
18 cups mixed salad greens (spinach, green leaf, Boston, Romaine)
2 cups cottage cheese mixed with 1 cup Ricotta cheese
2 cups diced tomatoes
2 cups finely grated carrots
¼ cup slivered black olives
18 spinach leaves
6 radish roses (make perpendicular cuts to form petals around the outside of the radish, then place in cold water to open petals)
18 diamond-shaped petals cut from a zucchini

Method:

1. Place 3 cups of salad greens in 6 individual 1-quart-capacity salad bowls. Scoop a portion of cottage cheese into the center, and alternate 3 mounds of diced tomatoes and 3 mounds of shredded carrots around the cottage cheese. Sprinkle tomatoes with black olives.

2. Garnish the salad by placing 3 spinach leaves at the base of the cheese mound, and placing a radish rose with 3 zucchini petals on top of the cheese mound.

3. Serve with your choice of dressing on the side (recipes on pages 42-44).

Photograph on page 225

Phoenician Salmon Salad

(Serves 6)

Ingredients:
24 ounces cooked salmon
2 teaspoons finely minced ginger
½ cup mayonnaise or ¼ cup mayonnaise and ¼ cup 2% yogurt
2 tablespoons lime juice
¾ teaspoon salt
¼ teaspoon cayenne pepper
2½ cups julienne carrots
1 cup julienne red bell peppers
6 ¼-inch slices purple onion
36 honeydew melon balls
6 cantelope melon balls
1½ tablespoons dried currants
30 whole spinach leaves
6 sprigs dill weed
6 radishes, cut into thin slices
12 orchid petals
6 basil leaves

Method:

1. Combine the first 6 ingredients to make the salmon salad. Set aside in the refrigerator to cool.

2. Blanch the julienne carrots and peppers in boiling water for approximately 30 seconds, making sure that they are tender but still crunchy. Set aside in the refrigerator to cool.

3. Arrange the ingredients on 6 dinner plates according to the photograph. Plates can be prepared ahead of time at this point, covered with plastic wrap, and refrigerated until serving time.

Photograph on page 175

Vegetable-Bean Soup

(Serves 6)

Ingredients:
1 carrot, peeled and cut into coin-size pieces
1 onion, diced
1 stalk celery, diced
1 tablespoon olive oil
6 cups chicken stock or canned chicken consommé
⅔ cup cooked or canned garbanzo beans
⅔ cup cooked or canned pinto beans
⅔ cup fresh or frozen cauliflower buds
1 tomato, peeled and diced
⅔ cup fresh or frozen green beans
⅔ cup fresh or frozen green peas
salt and pepper, to taste
½ cup fresh spinach leaves, torn into bite-size pieces
¼ cup thinly sliced red cabbage
¼ cup thinly sliced red bell pepper
¼ cup small sprigs parsley

Method:
1. In a large pot, cook the carrots, onions, and celery in the olive oil until the onions are soft and translucent. Add the stock, garbanzo and pinto beans, cauliflower, and tomato. Simmer on a low flame for approximately 1 hour. To retain the fresh green color of the green beans and peas, add and cook them 10 minutes before serving time. Season with salt and pepper.

2. To serve, pour into soup bowls, and sprinkle with spinach leaves, red cabbage, red pepper, and parsley.

Photograph on page 226

Orange Slaw Salad

(Serves 6)

Ingredients: 1 head red cabbage, sliced
1 small carrot, peeled and cut into small rectangular pieces
½ red bell pepper, cut into julienne pieces
½ green bell pepper, cut into julienne pieces
1 small can mandarin orange segments or 2 oranges, cut into segments (peel oranges and cut out segments between the membranes with a paring knife)
6 sprigs Mache lettuce or baby spinach or watercress
6 sprigs dill weed
12 orchid petals

Method: 1.   Place a 2-ounce mound of red cabbage onto each plate. Garnish the top of the cabbage with carrot, bell peppers, and oranges. Garnish the plate with the Mache lettuce, dill weed, and orchid petals.

2.   Serve with your choice of dressing on the side (recipes on pages 42-44).

Photograph on page 236

Tomato and Spinach Salad

(Serves 6)

Ingredients:
4 cups finely sliced, fresh spinach
6 Italian plum tomatoes, sliced
9 cherry tomatoes, cut into quarters
30 yellow pear tomatoes
30 fresh oregano or marjoram leaves
6 sprigs fresh basil
Roquefort Cheese Dressing

Method:

1. Place ⅔ of a cup of spinach on each of 6 large salad or dinner plates. Cover each serving of the spinach with 5 cherry tomato quarters, 5 pear tomatoes, and 5 oregano or marjoram leaves. Lay out a sliced plum tomato along the side of the spinach, and garnish with a sprig of basil.

2. Serve with Roquefort Cheese Dressing on the side (recipe on page 42).

Photograph on page 181

Cinderella Salad

(Serves 6)

Ingredients: 1 medium-sized spaghetti squash or 4½ cups finely grated cheese
6 canned or fresh bing cherries
12 cups prepared tossed greens in bite-sized pieces (a mix of spinach and
  Boston lettuce)
3 cups finely grated carrots
½ cup toasted cashew nuts (bake cashews in 400 degree oven for
  12 minutes)
½ cup honey-roasted pecans (toss the pecans with 1 teaspoon of honey,
  lay out on a lightly oiled sheet pan, and bake for 15 minutes in a
  400 degree oven)
¼ cup currants
18 Radicchio lettuce leaf cups
36 strawberries

Method:
1. Boil the spaghetti squash for approximately 1 hour until tender. Squash
   is tender when an inserted knife comes out without any resistance. Cut
   the squash in half, and remove the seeds. Scrape out the interior with a
   spoon, and set aside in the refrigerator to cool.

2. Place a bing cherry (the hidden surprise) in the center of 6
   9-inch plates. Cover the cherries with 2 cups of prepared salad greens.

3. Place ½ cup of grated carrots on top of the salad greens, and sprinkle
   the top with nuts and currants.

4. Alternate 3 mounds of spaghetti squash and 3 Radicchio lettuce leaf
   cups around the salad greens. Garnish with 6 strawberries set between
   the mounds of spaghetti squash and the Radicchio cups.

5. Serve with Magic Wands (recipe on page 106), and your choice of
   dressing on the side (recipes on pages 42-44).

Photograph on page 163

Seafood

Shrimp and Scallops Marjorie

shrimp and scallops served in a spinach sauce

(Serves 6)

Ingredients:
¾ cup chicken stock or canned chicken consommé
¾ cup whole milk
3 tablespoons dry sherry
3 tablespoons unbleached, all-purpose flour
¼ teaspoon cayenne pepper
¼ teaspoon curry powder
2 cups fresh spinach
1½ pounds large, shelled, and deveined shrimp
1 pound bay scallops
3 tablespoons safflower oil
4 sprigs parsley
4 to 6 small orchids

Method:

1. In a saucepan, combine the chicken stock, milk, sherry, flour, cayenne pepper, and curry powder. Stir, and cook over high heat until the sauce comes to a boil and thickens. Lower the flame, and simmer for approximately 15 minutes. Then remove the sauce from the burner, and let it cool for approximately 10 minutes. Combine the sauce and spinach in a blender, and purée for approximately 10 seconds. Pour the spinach sauce back into the saucepan, and set aside until serving time.

2. Over a medium-high heat in a large skillet, cook the shrimp for a few minutes in 1½ tablespoons oil until the center of the shrimp is no longer translucent. Set shrimp aside. Repeat the same procedure for the scallops, cooking them only a minute or two while leaving the center of the scallops slightly raw. Set scallops aside.

3. To serve, heat the spinach sauce, taking care not to cook the sauce too long in order to preserve the bright green color of the fresh spinach. Pour the sauce on the bottom of a heated serving platter. Over high heat, quickly reheat the shrimp and scallops in a skillet. Roll them out into the center of the platter on top of the spinach sauce, and garnish the sides of the platter with parsley sprigs and orchids.

Photograph on page 231

Almond-Dusted Swordfish

(Serves 6)

Ingredients:
6 5-ounce Swordfish steaks, cut 1-inch in thickness
2 tablespoons melted butter or margarine
¼ cup chopped, toasted almonds
¼ cup sourdough bread crumbs
¾ teaspoon chopped mint leaves
⅛ teaspoon cayenne pepper
⅛ teaspoon black pepper
5 tablespoons butter or margarine
1½ tablespoons lime juice
2 teaspoons grated lime peel
2 tablespoons chopped green onion
6 lemon wedges
6 sprigs parsley

Method:

1. Preheat oven to 450 degrees.

2. Place the fish on a nonstick or lightly buttered baking pan, and brush with melted butter.

3. Combine the almonds, bread crumbs, mint, cayenne pepper, and black pepper. Sprinkle the mixture on top of the fish. Bake fish for approximately 10 minutes until the flesh of the fish just begins to flake.

4. While the fish is baking, heat the butter and lime juice in a saucepan. Place the fish on serving plates. Add the lime peel and green onion to the hot butter and lime mixture. Without any further heating, pour a tablespoon of the sauce over each piece of fish.

5. Garnish with a lemon wedge and a sprig of parsley.

Photograph on page 235

Fillet of Sole Miro

sole fillet basted with a white wine sauce, served with snow peas and green onions

(Serves 6)

Ingredients:
¾ cup fish stock or clam juice
¾ cup whole milk
¼ cup Chablis or dry vermouth
3 tablespoons unbleached, all-purpose flour
¼ teaspoon cayenne pepper
6 4-ounce pieces sole fillets
salt and pepper
¾ pound Chinese snow peas
1 tablespoon olive oil
1 cup of the tops of green onions cut into 1½-inch pieces
3 limes
parsley
red, yellow, and green bell pepper
black olives
a few chives
chervil or parsley

Method:

1. In a saucepan, combine the fish stock, milk, wine, flour, and cayenne pepper. Stir, and cook over a high heat until the sauce comes to a boil and thickens. Lower the flame, and simmer for approximately 20 minutes. The sauce should be thick enough to lightly coat the back of a spoon. Cover, and keep the sauce warm over a low flame.

2. Lay out the fish on a lightly oiled baking pan, and sprinkle lightly with salt and pepper. Bake in a preheated 350 degree oven for 7 to 10 minutes until the flesh of the fish just begins to separate.

3. While the fish is cooking, cut the limes in half by making zig-zag cuts through the center of each lime. Place half of a lime on each of 6 large dinner plates, and garnish with 2 sprigs of parsley.

4. In a skillet over high heat, quickly stir fry the snow peas in the oil for a couple of minutes. Fold in the green onion tops, and portion out onto the plates. Place the cooked fish on the plates, and cover with a couple of tablespoons of sauce.

(Recipe continued on next page.)

5. Garnish the sauce with cut pieces of bell pepper, black olives, chives, and chervil as in the photograph. Serve at once while still hot.

Photograph on page 179

Cracked Alaskan King Crab Legs

(Serves 6)

Ingredients: 3 pounds Alaskan King crab legs (these crab legs are often marketed frozen and already cooked)
1 lime, cut into 8 wedges
parsley, dill sprigs, and a few fresh flowers
2 tablespoons chopped garlic
¼ pound butter
2 tablespoons white wine
½ cup chicken stock or canned chicken consommé
2 tablespoons chopped, toasted pistachio nuts

Method: 1. Thaw crab legs. With a sharp knife cut the legs in half lengthwise. Lay out on a baking pan, and cover with aluminum foil.

2. If the crab legs are already cooked, heat in a preheated 375 degree oven for approximately 8 minutes; if uncooked, leave them in the oven for approximately 15 to 20 minutes.

3. Transfer the legs to a large serving platter. Place lime wedges between crab legs, and garnish the platter with parsley, dill, and flowers.

4. In a saucepan, cook the garlic in the butter until there is some browning around the outer edges of the garlic. Add the wine and chicken stock. Simmer for a few minutes. Pour the sauce into a serving dish, mix in the pistachio nuts, and serve on the side with the crab legs.

Photograph on page 211

Culinary Quiz

The following is a quiz on food, wine, and related bits of culinary trivia.

For fun, let's see how well you can do:

1. **Bouquet Garni**
   - (a) The most important item on a buffet
   - (b) A term used to describe wine
   - (c) A mixture of herbs

2. **Eggs Benedict**
   - (a) A poached egg served on toasted English muffin with a slice of ham and covered with Hollandaise sauce
   - (b) Baked eggs served in a ramekin with cheese, spinach, and croutons
   - (c) An asparagus and mushroom omelette covered with Mornay sauce

3. **Steele**
   - (a) An instrument used for honing knives
   - (b) A 50% discount on all groceries
   - (c) A thin flexible knife used to fillet fish

4. **Chutney**
   - (a) A tropical fruit resembling bananas
   - (b) Small, sweet, thin-shelled nuts from pine cones
   - (c) A pungent relish made of fruits, spices, and herbs

5. **Wok**
   - (a) A cooking utensil used for pounding meat
   - (b) A round Chinese cooking skillet
   - (c) A slang word for over-cooked food

(Culinary Quiz continued on next page.)

6. **Capers**
   (a) Pickled buds from a Mediterranean shrub
   (b) Onion-like plant whose clustered bulbs resemble garlic, but are milder
   (c) Smoked young fish

7. **Stilton**
   (a) A sourdough rye bread
   (b) Rich dark beer brewed from wheat and barley
   (c) An English bleu cheese

8. **Brut**
   (a) The thin, brown, outer covering of the wheat grain
   (b) A bartender or waiter who removes your drink when it is one-quarter full
   (c) The term that designates an extra dry champagne

9. **Chicken Lobster**
   (a) A description of a flavorful lobster
   (b) Young lobster weighing about a pound
   (c) Stanford University's latest genetic recombination

10. **Stock**
    (a) A thick soup made with beans and vegetables
    (b) The liquid in which meat, fish, or vegetables have been simmered that is used as a basis for soup, gravy, and sauces.
    (c) A butcher's block that is at least twelve inches in thickness

11. **Escoffier**
    (a) The last name of a famous French chef
    (b) A brown sauce with truffles and burgundy wine
    (c) A long, oval, copper cooking utensil used mostly for poaching large fish

12. **Saké**
    (a) A noncaloric substitute for sugar
    (b) Raw fish served on a wooden plank
    (c) A Japanese wine made from rice

13. **Braising**
    (a) Cooking in a very hot pan
    (b) Cooking with a small amount of liquid
    (c) Placing underneath a broiler to heat food to crispness just before serving

(Culinary Quiz continued on next page.)

14. **Paella**

    (a) Spanish dish made with rice, vegetables, meat, and seafood
    (b) Small, oval fruit with purple skin and yellow flesh
    (c) Indian fried bread

15. **Scungilli**

    (a) An Italian dish made with whelk or conch
    (b) An Italian dish made with squid
    (c) What an Italian waiter will say when dissatisfied with his gratuity

16. **Mise en place**

    (a) A French term that describes an unorganized kitchen
    (b) A French term meaning the preparation is ready up to the point of cooking
    (c) A term used in French restaurants meaning the guests for dinner have arrived

17. **John Dory**

    (a) A flavorful salt-water fish often used in the preparation of bouillabaisse
    (b) Author of *A Thousand And One Ways To Cook Seaweed For Stress Reduction*
    (c) Author of *Joy of Cooking*

18. **Flambé**

    (a) A custard dessert with caramel topping
    (b) Food dressed or served with flaming liquor
    (c) Flamboyant food service

19. **Quiche**

    (a) An open custard tart
    (b) An affectionate greeting from a maitre d'
    (c) A small rum cake

20. **Naturally Sparkling Water**

    (a) Water that, when underground, contains enough carbon dioxide to make it bubbly
    (b) Water that has been filtered and carbonated, and to which minerals are added
    (c) Good old-fashioned seltzer

21. **Kummel**

    (a) A Russian liqueur made from caraway
    (b) A dark Bavarian bread with cornmeal and rye
    (c) The syrup remaining from sugar cane juice after sucrose crystallization

(Culinary Quiz continued on next page.)

22. **Souvlakia**
    (a) Very thin pastry sheets with a sweet, savory filling, rolled up and baked
    (b) A spinach pie
    (c) Meat marinated in olive oil, lemon juice, and herbs, then skewered and grilled

23. **Jicama**
    (a) A crisp, slightly sweet-tasting Mexican root vegetable resembling a turnip
    (b) A large wine bottle with the capacity of six ordinary bottles
    (c) A Cajun dish made from rice and seafood, served Creole style

24. **Schmalz**
    (a) A small, highly-prized North American game bird
    (b) Melted fat
    (c) A plum brandy

25. **Hush puppies**
    (a) Deep-fried cornmeal dumplings, sometimes flavored with chopped onions
    (b) Miniature hot dogs barbecued Southern-style
    (c) A term used to designate a very fine caviar

Scoring Instructions

Give yourself one point for each correct answer:

1) (c)	6) (a)	11) (a)	16) (b)	21) (a)
2) (a)	7) (c)	12) (c)	17) (a)	22) (c)
3) (a)	8) (c)	13) (b)	18) (b)	23) (a)
4) (c)	9) (b)	14) (a)	19) (a)	24) (b)
5) (b)	10) (b)	15) (a)	20) (a)	25) (a)

If you have scored:

21 - 25   You are a gastronomical connoisseur
16 - 20   You enjoy the pleasures of the palate
11 - 15   You can use a few more cookbooks in your library
 6 - 10   Your favorite eating establishment is McDonald's
 0 - 5   You eat only to survive

Shrimp Fantasia

barbecued shrimp with spinach noodles, zucchini, pineapple, and oyster mushrooms

(Serves 6)

Ingredients:

12 ounces spinach noodles
36 large shrimp, peeled and deveined
1 cup barbecue sauce (see recipe on next page)
36 finger-sized cut pieces zucchini, sprinkled with Parmesan cheese
18 1-inch diced pieces fresh pineapple
2 cups strong flavored chicken stock or canned chicken consommé
18 large oyster mushrooms
½ cup julienne cut red bell pepper
6 sprigs fresh basil

Method:

1. Cook noodles in lightly salted boiling water until tender but still slightly chewy (al dente).

2. Toss the shrimp with barbecue sauce, and cook over a charcoal broiler or under an oven broiler for a couple of minutes on each side until the shrimp are no longer opaque in the center. Take care not to overcook the shrimp. Set aside.

3. Cook the zucchini and pineapple over a charcoal broiler or under an oven broiler until tender with edges browned and crunchy. Set aside.

4. Bring the chicken stock to a boil. Add the oyster mushrooms, and blanch for approximately 10 seconds until slightly wilted.

5. Place a bed of noodles on each of 6 heated dinner plates. Alternate 6 pieces of shrimp with 6 pieces of zucchini around the outside of the noodles. Form a cup with 3 oyster mushrooms in the center of each bed of noodles, and fill with 3 pieces of pineapple. Sprinkle the top with julienne red pepper. Baste with hot chicken stock, and garnish with a sprig of basil.

Photograph on page 213

Barbecue Sauce

(Makes 1¼ cups sauce)

Ingredients: ½ cup soy sauce
¼ cup honey
¼ cup apricot preserves
¼ cup chile sauce
2 teaspoons Coleman's mustard or other hot powdered mustard

Method: 1. Mix together.

Twelve Seasons Salt

Use this exotic seasoning mixture as an extra condiment to accompany your salt and pepper shakers.

(Makes 1½ cups seasoned salt)

Ingredients: ½ cup dried parsley flakes
3 tablespoons dried tarragon
2 tablespoons dried basil
2 tablespoons rosehips (for easy availability, remove from rosehips tea bags)
2 tablespoons garlic salt
2 tablespoons onion salt
1 tablespoon fennel seed
1 tablespoon paprika
1 tablespoon curry powder
1 tablespoon grated lemon rind
1 teaspoon cayenne pepper
1 teaspoon saffron

Method: 1. Place the ingredients in a food processor or a blender. Process for approximately 10 seconds until the seasoning salt can pour through a salt shaker with large holes. For best storage, refrigerate, or freeze in a container or a jar with a tight-fitting cover.

Photograph on page 220

Twelve Seasons Lobster Tails

(Serves 6)

Ingredients:
6 8-ounce frozen Australian or New Zealand lobster tails
olive oil
Twelve Seasons Salt (see recipe on previous page)
¾ pound yellow straight-neck squash, cut into julienne pieces
¾ pound zucchini squash, cut into julienne pieces
1 large red bell pepper, cut into julienne pieces
salt and white pepper, to taste
6 lemon halves, garnished with a cut-out piece of black olive and a sprig of parsley to resemble a flower pot
6 Radicchio lettuce leaves or red cabbage leaves
fresh parsley sprigs
fresh chives

Method:

1. Thaw the lobster tails. With a sharp knife, cut through the top shell and the meat of each tail. Open up the tail, and gently pull the meat out from the shell, leaving only a small portion at the tip of the tail intact. Close the shell, and lay the meat over the closed shell. Lay out the tails on a baking sheet, brush with olive oil and sprinkle with Twelve Seasons Salt. The lobster tails can be prepared at this point, and refrigerated ahead of time. Twenty minutes before serving time, place the prepared tray of lobster tails in a preheated 400 degree oven for approximately 20 minutes. Lobster is done when the center of the thickest part of the meat just begins to lose its shiny, raw consistency and takes on a firmer, milky-white appearance.

2. While the lobster tails are cooking, brush a heated skillet with olive oil, and stir-fry julienne vegetables over a medium-high heat for approximately 1 minute, until crisp with a touch of browning. Season with salt and pepper.

3. Place the cooked lobster tails on individual dinner plates. Place a Radicchio lettuce leaf on each plate, and fill with vegetables. Garnish the plates with lemon, parsley sprigs, and fresh chives.

Photograph on page 174

Half of Tuna Salad Sandwich

(Makes 6 half-sandwiches)

Ingredients:
1 13-ounce can water-packed Albacore tuna fish
¼ cup mayonnaise
¼ cup 2% yogurt
2 tablespoons Chinese rice vinegar
½ cup diced celery
1 tablespoon chopped parsley
6 slices whole wheat bread
1 package radish sprouts
6 strawberries
18 Belgium endive leaves
30 pickle chips
6 sprigs dill weed

Method:
1. In a bowl, break up the tuna fish, and mix it with the mayonnaise, yogurt, vinegar, celery, and parsley.

2. Divide the mixture onto 3 slices of bread, flatten down with a spatula, and cover with remaining three slices of bread. Cut sandwiches in half on the diagonal, and place a few sprouts in the center of each half-sandwich.

3. Place the sandwiches on plates. Garnish with a strawberry, 3 endive leaves, pickle chips, and dill weed.

4. Serve with Saffron Soup (recipe on page 19).

Photograph on page 181

Good eating habits happen

when our consciousness is no longer dominated

by addictions and demands

and we experience the table before us

as a parade of preferences.

Meat

and

Poultry

Would that you could live on the fragrance of the earth,
and like an air plant be sustained by the light.

But since you must kill to eat, and rob the newly born of its mother's
milk to quench your thirst, let it then be an act of worship.

And let your board stand an altar on which the pure and the innocent of forest
and plain are sacrificed for that which is purer and still more innocent in man.

When you kill a beast say to him in your heart,
"By the same power that slays you, I too am slain; and I too shall be consumed.
For the law that delivered you into my hand shall deliver me into a mightier hand.
Your blood and my blood is naught but the sap that feeds the tree of heaven."

And when you crush an apple with your teeth, say to it in your heart,
"Your seeds shall live in my body,
And the buds of your tomorrow shall blossom in my heart,
And your fragrance shall be my breath,
And together we shall rejoice through all the seasons."

— Kahlil Gibran

Barbecued Pork Tenderloin with Orange Slaw Salad

(Serves 6)

Ingredients: ½ cup soy sauce
¼ cup honey
¼ cup apricot preserves
¼ cup chile sauce
2 teaspoons Coleman's mustard or other hot powdered mustard
2 pounds pork tenderloin, trimmed of all visible fat
1 tablespoon vegetable oil
sesame seeds

Method:
1. Purée the soy sauce, honey, apricot preserves, chile sauce, and mustard in a blender or food processor. Marinate tenderloin in sauce for at least 3 hours or overnight.

2. Remove pork from barbecue sauce. Pour sauce in a saucepan, and begin to heat on a low burner.

3. Dry the pork with a towel, and rub on the vegetable oil. Cook over or under a preheated charcoal or oven broiler for approximately 15 to 20 minutes turning on occasion with a pair of tongs until the internal temperature measures 160 degrees on a meat thermometer.

4. Let the pork rest for a few minutes, then slice into pieces ½-inch in thickness. Portion out 4 ounces for an entrée (2½ to 3 ounces for a salad or an appetizer) on each plate that has been prepared with Orange Slaw Salad (recipe on page 38).

5. Bring the barbecue sauce to a boil. Spoon sauce over the sliced pork, sprinkle with sesame seeds, and serve.

Photograph on page 236

Chicken and Celery Bisteeya

marinated strips of chicken breast baked in fillo dough

(Serves 6)

Ingredients: 6 boned and skinned chicken breasts (approximately 24 ounces), cut into strips
¾ cup chopped celery
3 tablespoons white raisins
1½ tablespoons chopped parsley
1 tablespoon lemon juice
1 tablespoon olive oil
1 teaspoon minced ginger
1 teaspoon minced garlic
1 teaspoon salt
½ teaspoon turmeric
½ teaspoon coriander
½ teaspoon cayenne pepper
6 10-inch by 10-inch sheets of fillo dough
confectioners sugar
ground cinnamon
12 Belgium endive lettuce leaves
18 strawberries

Method: 1. Mix the first 12 ingredients together, and let marinate for at least 3 hours, preferably overnight.

2. Preheat oven to 400 degrees.

3. Portion out the chicken mixture into the center of each sheet of fillo dough. Bring the corners of the dough together, and pinch them to close over the chicken mixture. Lay out on a nonstick or lightly oiled baking pan. Bake for approximately 15 to 20 minutes. Using a paring knife, make a small incision on the bottom of one bisteeya to be sure the chicken has been cooked through.

4. Sprinkle the bisteeya with confectioners sugar and cinnamon. Place 1 on each of 6 serving plates, and garnish each plate with 2 Belgium endive lettuce leaves, 3 strawberries, and a portion of the Cherry Tomato and Bean Salad (recipe on page 19).

Photograph on page 218

Veal Patties with Mushrooms and Chervil

(Serves 6)

Ingredients:
2 slices rye bread
1½ cups veal or chicken stock
1 teaspoon minced garlic
1 teaspoon olive oil
1½ pounds lean ground veal
1 egg
2 tablespoons Parmesan cheese
½ teaspoon black pepper
olive oil
1 pound large mushrooms, sliced ¼-inch in thickness
½ cup red wine such as a Cabernet or Zinfandel
small red pepper, cut julienne
2 tablespoons chopped chervil or parsley
fresh spinach leaves

Method:

1. Soak the bread in ½ cup veal or chicken stock. Sauté the garlic in the teaspoon of olive oil for approximately 30 seconds until golden brown. Add the garlic and oil to the bread. Add the veal, egg, Parmesan cheese, and pepper. Mix, and form into 6 patties.

2. Lightly brush the bottom of a skillet with olive oil. Cook veal patties over medium-high heat for approximately 3 minutes on each side, trying to brown the outside while leaving the center of the patties slightly pink. Set patties aside, and keep warm.

3. Brush the skillet with some more olive oil, and sauté the mushrooms, taking care to not overcrowd the skillet so that the mushrooms will brown on the outside and still be fresh and crisp. Set mushrooms aside, and keep warm.

4. Add the red wine to the skillet along with the remaining cup of veal or chicken stock. Boil over high heat until the mixture is reduced to 1 cup.

5. Place a cooked veal patty in the center of each of 6 plates. Surround patties with mushrooms. Garnish the top of the patties with red pepper and chervil. Surround the plate with spinach leaves. Pour a couple of tablespoons of the hot wine sauce on top of each veal patty, and serve.

Photograph on page 219

Chicken Breasts Sheila

---

sautéed chicken breasts on a bed of saffron rice, surrounded by sliced zucchini

(Serves 6)

Ingredients: 4 cups chicken stock or canned chicken consommé
½ teaspoon whole saffron
1 bay leaf
1 clove garlic
1 tablespoon olive oil
1 medium onion, finely chopped
2 cups short-grain brown rice
2 tablespoons chopped parsley
salt and white pepper, to taste
6 chicken breasts, boned and skinned
2 zucchini, cut into ¼-inch slices
olive oil
apple bird (illustration on next page)
alfalfa sprouts
2 sprigs watercress
chutney (preferably London Pub's Major Grey Chutney)

Method: 1.   Simmer the stock with the saffron, bay leaf, and the clove of garlic for approximately 20 minutes.

2.   In a skillet, sauté the onion in the tablespoon of olive oil until there is some browning around the edges. Add the rice, and cook, stirring until the rice turns opaque.

3.   Discard the saffron, bay leaf, and garlic, and add the stock to the rice in the skillet. Cover the skillet, and cook over low heat for approximately 60 minutes until the rice has absorbed all of the liquid. Remove from heat and mix in the chopped parsley.

4.   While the rice is cooking, lightly salt and pepper the chicken breasts and the sliced zucchini. Lightly coat a large frying pan with olive oil. Over medium-high heat sauté the chicken breasts for approximately 2 minutes on each side. The breasts are perfectly cooked when there is some browning on the outside, they still feel soft, and a trace of pink is left in the center. Set breasts aside.

(Recipe continued on next page.)

Veal Medallions with Red Peppercorns, Fresh Thyme, and Truffles

(Serves 6)

Ingredients:
1 teaspoon chopped garlic
1 tablespoon butter or margarine
2 cups strongly flavored veal stock, made from veal bones
1½ tablespoons cornstarch
1 tablespoon red peppercorns
1 small black truffle, cut into thin slivers
2 tablespoons Cognac
1½ pounds boned-out veal loin
salt and pepper
olive oil
1 teaspoon fresh thyme
sprig of thyme that has been blanched in boiling water for 10 seconds to bring out the aroma and bright green color

Method:

1. In a saucepan, cook the garlic in the butter for approximately 30 seconds, taking care not to burn it. Mix the veal stock with the cornstarch; add to the saucepan, and bring to a boil. Add the peppercorns, truffle, and Cognac. Cook for a few minutes, then set aside on a low burner while preparing the veal.

2. Trim the veal loin of all excess fat. Cut against the grain into slices ¼-inch in thickness. Sprinkle slices lightly with salt and pepper. Lightly coat a large skillet with olive oil. Sauté the veal over medium-high heat for approximately 20 seconds on each side. Veal medallions should be browned on the outside and have a slightly pink tinge in the center. Place the cooked veal in a overlapping row on a large, heated, oval serving platter.

3. Pour the prepared sauce into the skillet in which the veal has been cooked. With a wooden spoon, scrape up scraps of veal that are clinging to the bottom of the skillet. Add the teaspoon of thyme to the sauce, stir, and heat for approximately 1 minute, then pour the sauce over the prepared veal.

4. Garnish the platter with the sprig of thyme, and serve.

Photograph on page 227

HOW TO COOK A TURKEY

by

Brad

Take off the feathers. Take off the skin. Put it in the oven. Cook 20 or 10 minutes. Eat it.

Roast Rack of Lamb Gregory

(Serves 6)

Ingredients: 3 half racks lamb, trimmed French style
2 tablespoons minced garlic
2 tablespoons olive oil
1 tablespoon coriander
1 teaspoon paprika
1 teaspoon cumin
¾ teaspoon salt
1 cup chicken or beef stock or canned chicken or beef consommé
fresh watercress sprigs

Method:

1. Lay out lamb racks in a roasting pan. Make a paste with the garlic, oil, coriander, paprika, cumin, and salt. Rub the paste all over the lamb racks, and refrigerate for a few hours or overnight.

2. Roast the lamb racks in a preheated 325 degree oven for approximately 20 minutes on each side until the internal temperature, when measured with a meat thermometer, is 145 degrees. (It is best to use a thin Taylor brand thermometer to prevent loss of juice.) Set aside racks until serving time.

3. Add stock or consommé to the roasting pan, and scrape all the brown bits sticking to the bottom of the pan. Transfer the liquid to a saucepan, bring to a boil, cook for a few minutes, then strain through paper towels or a fine cheesecloth. Keep warm.

4. Before serving, place lamb racks underneath a preheated broiler to brown and heat. Cut racks into individual serving chops. Arrange chops with the bones criss-crossing on a heated serving platter. Baste chops with some of the lamb juice. Serve the remaining juice on the side in a sauce boat. Garnish the serving platter with watercress.

5. Serve with Red Potatoes (recipe on page 88) and Asparagus (recipe on page 92).

Photograph on page 188

Chicken Klotz-Reilly

Chicken Klotz-Reilly is named after a Phoenix artist whose artwork often mixes clay figures, beads, foil, teeth, lace, and whatever seems to come into her mind.

Her work is a bit exotic, and so is this dish that was inspired from her collage above my dining room buffet.

(Serves 6)

Ingredients:
6 boned and skinned chicken breasts (approximately 1½ pounds), cut into strips
1 cup chopped celery
3 tablespoons white raisins
1½ tablespoons chopped parsley
1 tablespoon lemon juice
2 tablespoons olive oil
1 tablespoon soy sauce
1 teaspoon minced ginger
1 teaspoon minced garlic
1 teaspoon salt
½ teaspoon turmeric
½ teaspoon coriander
½ teaspoon cayenne pepper
6 apples, peeled, cored, and chopped
2 cups apple juice
12 5-inch by 5-inch sheets of fillo dough
6 cups finely shredded, fresh spinach
12 slices plum tomatoes, grilled in a hot skillet
18 yellow pear tomatoes, cut in half, and grilled in a hot skillet
6 Radicchio lettuce leaf cups
6 sprigs of basil or watercress
confectioners sugar
cinnamon

Method:
1. In a bowl, mix the first 13 ingredients together. Let marinate for at least 3 hours.

2. In a nonstick skillet over high heat, quickly sauté the chicken mixture for approximately 30 seconds, taking care not to overcook it. Refrigerate cooked chicken until chilled.

(Recipe continued on next page.)

3. In a saucepan, cook the apples in the apple juice until apples are tender and the juice is reduced to an applesauce consistency. Portion out 2 tablespoons of applesauce in the center of each sheet of filo dough. Bring the corners of the dough together and pinch above the applesauce. Lay out on a nonstick or lightly oiled baking pan. Bake in a preheated 400 degree oven for approximately 10 minutes until golden brown. Set aside until serving time.

4. Place a cup of spinach on 6 large dinner plates. Portion out the chicken mixture on top of the spinach. Line the sides of the spinach with the grilled tomatoes. Garnish the plates with a Radicchio lettuce leaf cup filled with basil. At this point, plates may be made ahead of time, covered with plastic wrap, and refrigerated.

5. Before serving, heat the filo dough pastries in a 300 degree oven for a couple of minutes. Sprinkle them lightly with confectioners sugar and cinnamon, and place 2 on each serving plate. Serve with Soy and Sesame Seed Dressing on the side (recipe on page 43).

Photograph on page 203

Charcoal-Broiled Hamburgers with Trimmings

(Serves 6)

Ingredients: 2 pounds ground sirloin or chuck, 80% lean
½ teaspoon freshly ground pepper
2 pounds potatoes, cleaned and sliced lengthwise with skin left on
2 tablespoons vegetable oil
6 sesame seed hamburger buns
6 Boston lettuce leaves
6 onion slices
6 tomato slices
2 dill pickles, cut into julienne pieces
1 red bell pepper, cut into julienne pieces

(Recipe continued on next page)

Ingredients continued:

1½ cups watermelon balls

1½ cups green grapes

6 Savoy or other lettuce leaves

6 French radish roses (make perpendicular cuts to form petals around the outside of the radish, then place in cold water to open petals)

Method:

1. Preheat a charcoal broiler. It is important to have an intense heat to sear the burgers which will trap the juice inside while giving the outside a brown crust.

2. Using your hands, gently mix the ground beef with the pepper. Shape into 6 patties 1-inch in thickness.

3. Mix the potatoes with the vegetable oil. Lay them out on the charcoal broiler, and cook the potatoes until they are tender while turning them with tongs so that they will cook evenly on each side.

4. When the potatoes are just about done cooking, add the prepared hamburger patties to the broiler, and cook for approximately 3 minutes on each side for medium-rare or 4 minutes on each side for medium.

5. A minute before the hamburgers are done, split the buns, and place on the broiler to toast.

6. Place the toasted bun on a plate with the hamburger. Garnish the top of the bun with a Boston lettuce leaf, a slice of onion, tomato, julienne pickle, and bell pepper. Place grilled potatoes on the plate with the watermelon balls and grapes atop a Savoy lettuce leaf, and garnish with a radish rose. For an added treat, try serving the hamburgers with Roquefort Cheese Dressing (recipe on page 42) or Green Cucumber Salsa (recipe on page 43).

Photograph on page 241

Vegetables

and

Starches

Millet with Carrots, Ginger, and Chives

Millet, a tasty, non-glutenous grain native to Africa and Asia, has been cultivated in dry, poor soil for millennia as an important protein staple, but in the United States, where it is grown on the western plain, it is used mostly for animal fodder.

A quick nutritional comparison to rice shows that ounce-for-ounce, millet has 90 calories and 3 grams of protein compared to rice's 110 calories and 2 grams of protein. As you can see, the A.S.P.C.A. should be proud of us.

(Serves 6)

Ingredients:
2 tablespoons olive oil
2 cups millet
4 cups boiling water
1¼ cups finely diced carrots
1 tablespoon minced ginger
½ cup chopped chives
salt and white pepper, to taste
a few thin slivers yellow bell pepper
a few thin slivers red bell pepper
a few chives
parsley
5 or 6 radish roses (make perpendicular cuts to form petals around the outside of the radish, then place in cold water to open petals)

Method:

1. Heat the oil in a heavy skillet. Add the millet, and toast gently until the grain is a light tan color. Add the boiling water, cover, and cook for approximately 25 minutes on a low flame until all the water is absorbed.

2. Remove the skillet from the burner. Add the carrots, ginger, and chives, then add salt and pepper.

3. Mound the millet mixture on a heated serving platter. Garnish the top with the bell peppers and chives, and the sides with parsley and radish roses.

Photograph on page 182

Tomato-Basil Noodles with Pistachio Nuts and Garlic

(Serves 6)

Ingredients:
¾ cup high-gluten flour or bread flour
1 cup unbleached, all-purpose flour
½ cup tomato sauce
1 egg
2 tablespoons chopped basil
3 quarts boiling water
3 tablespoons salt
5 tablespoons butter or margarine
½ cup pistachio nuts
2 teaspoons chopped garlic
freshly ground pepper
parsley sprigs

Method:

1. In a bowl, sift the flours together, and combine with the tomato sauce, egg, and basil. Mix until a dough is formed. Roll out on a lightly floured worktable, and knead with your hands for a few minutes until a smooth, soft dough is formed.

2. Divide the dough into quarters. With a rolling pin, roll out each piece 3- to 4-inches in width and ¼-inch in thickness. Let the rolled out pieces of dough dry for 10 to 15 minutes. Brush the surface flour off of the dough, and cut into ½-inch-wide noodles. Cook the noodles for approximately 3 minutes in 3 quarts of boiling water combined with 3 tablespoons of salt. Drain the noodles in a colander, and rinse off under cool, running water.

3. In a large skillet, heat the butter, add the pistachio nuts, and cook them for 1 minute. Add the garlic and noodles. Toss the ingredients in the skillet for a few minutes so that a good portion of the noodles have a chance to brown and become crunchy. Add some freshly ground pepper, and serve garnished with a sprig of parsley.

Photograph on page 177

Cleopatra's Platter

*broccoli, baby carrots, and braised red onions, accompanied by
brown and wild rice with slivered almonds*

(Serves 6)

Ingredients: 5 cups strongly flavored beef stock or canned beef consommé
1 cup long-grain brown rice
1 cup wild rice
2 tablespoons slivered almonds, toasted
1 teaspoon chopped chives
1½ pounds broccoli, trimmed into spears
30 baby carrots, peeled
1 tablespoon butter or margarine
1 large red onion, cut into 8 wedges
purple savoy lettuce leaves
2 sprigs basil

Method:

1. In a skillet, bring 4 cups of the beef stock to a boil. Rinse the rice under cold water, and drain well. Add rice, cover, and cook over low heat for approximately 50 minutes until the rice is tender. Fold in the almonds and chives.

2. While the rice is cooking, steam or boil the broccoli until tender but still a little crunchy. In a skillet with a tight-fitting lid, add the carrots, ½ cup beef stock and ½ tablespoon butter. Cover, and cook until the carrots are tender and the stock has reduced with the butter to a syrupy glaze. Repeat the same process with the red onions using the remaining ½ cup beef stock and ½ tablespoon butter.

3. Arrange rice and vegetables on a serving platter. Garnish with the savoy lettuce leaves and basil.

Photograph on page 187

Silver Dollar Blueberry Pancakes with Sliced Peaches

(Serves 6)

Ingredients:
1 cup whole wheat flour
¾ cup unbleached, all-purpose flour
½ cup corn meal
1½ teapoons baking soda
1 teaspoon salt
2 eggs
2 cups buttermilk
2 tablespoons vegetable oil
2 cups blueberries, fresh or frozen
2 peaches
small bouquet of fresh flowers
butter or margarine
maple syrup

Method:

1. In a bowl, mix the flours, corn meal, baking soda, and salt together. Add the eggs, buttermilk, and vegetable oil. Mix just until a lump-free batter is formed. Gently fold in the blueberries.

2. Preheat a nonstick griddle so that it is hot enough to make a drop of water bounce across the surface. Using a tablespoon, spoon out batter onto the griddle. Cook until pancakes are puffy and edges begin to brown. Flip over and cook the other side for approximately 1 minute.

3. Place the pancakes on a large serving platter. At this point, the platter can be covered with aluminum foil, and placed in a 200 degree oven to be kept warm until serving time.

4. Slice the peaches, and place them between the pancakes. Garnish the center with a fresh flower bouquet, and serve with butter and maple syrup on the side.

Photograph on page 184

Vegetables O'Keefe

(Serves 6)

Ingredients:
3 cups broccoli buds
1½ cups carrots, cut into julienne pieces 2-inches in length
1½ cups lima beans
1½ cups yellow and red bell peppers, cut into julienne pieces 2-inches in length
1½ cups black-eyed peas
1½ cups green beans, cut 2-inches in length
1½ cups kernel corn
12 pieces canned pimiento, cut 2½-inches in length
12 pieces green onion tops, cut 2½-inches in length and blanched in boiling water for 10 seconds
3 tablespoons butter or margarine, melted

Method:

1. Cook all of the vegetables and beans separately in the microwave oven or by steaming or boiling them until they are tender but still a little crunchy. Place a ½ cup portion of broccoli buds in the center of 6 large dinner plates. Neatly arrange ¼ cup portions of vegetables and beans around the broccoli according to the photograph. Garnish the carrots with 2 pieces of green onion, and garnish the green beans with 2 pieces of pimiento.

2. Cover the top of the prepared plates with aluminum foil. Keep warm in a 150 degree oven until serving time. Using a pastry brush, brush each plate with melted butter, and serve.

Photograph on page 216

Peach-Almond Granola

This nutritious and quick breakfast is high in fiber, protein, and complex carbohydrates, and comes with its own fruit. Place in a bowl, add milk, and "bon appetit."

(Makes 2 quarts granola)

Ingredients:
5 cups rolled oats (such as Quaker Old Fashioned Oats)
1 cup sliced almonds
½ cup wheat germ
½ cup sesame seeds
½ cup bran
¼ cup honey
½ tablespoon pure vanilla extract
1 teaspoon cinnamon
⅔ cup dried peaches or apricots

Method:
1. Preheat oven to 350 degrees.

2. In a shallow baking pan that has been lightly buttered or oiled, mix all of the ingredients together except the peaches.

3. Bake for approximately 45 minutes, stirring if necessary to make sure the mixture is being toasted uniformly. When done, let mixture cool, then add peaches.

4. Refrigerate or freeze granola in plastic bags or containers with tight-fitting lids to preserve freshness.

Photograph on page 178

Zucchini-Banana Muffins

These are deliciously moist muffins prepared without fats or oils.

Try substituting carrots, blueberries, apples, and other
fruits and vegetables in place of the zucchini.

(Makes 2 dozen muffins)

Ingredients:
3 cups whole wheat flour
½ cup corn meal
2 teaspoons baking soda
2 teaspoons cinnamon
1 teaspoon salt
½ cup white raisins
½ cup chopped pecans
¾ cup honey
⅔ cup buttermilk
⅔ cup mashed, well-ripened bananas
4 eggs, beaten
1 teaspoon pure vanilla extract
5 cups grated zucchini

Method:
1. Preheat oven to 375 degrees.

2. In a bowl, mix the flour, corn meal, baking soda, cinnamon, salt, raisins, and pecans together.

3. Add the remaining ingredients, and stir until well blended.

4. Portion out batter into nonstick or lightly oiled muffin tins. Bake for approximately 30 minutes.

Photograph on page 183

* * * * * * * *

The following is an interesting way to serve these muffins:

*You put them in the oven. Then put them in the refrigerator cause it's too hot.
And then you eat them. That's it!*

— Tyler Golden, age four

* * * * * * * *

Cooked Vegetable Platter

Varied shapes and colors make this vegetable platter
pleasing to the eye as well as to the palate.

(Serves 6)

Ingredients:
3 large carrots
3 large rutabagas
3 large zucchini
12 large pearl onions
12 radishes
1½ tablespoons butter or margarine
salt and white pepper, to taste
a couple fresh flowers for garnishing

Method:

1. Cut the carrots into finger-size pieces, and with a paring knife round out the edges of the cut carrots. Cut the rutabagas into 1-inch dice-size pieces. Cut the zucchini into quarters lengthwise, and then into 2½-inch pieces. With a paring knife, round out the edges of the zucchini to form oval-shaped pieces.

2. Steam, boil, or microwave the vegetables separately until each vegetable is tender but still a little crunchy. Set aside vegetables until serving time.

3. Melt the butter in a large skillet. Add the vegetables, and toss them around in the butter. Season with salt and white pepper. Roll out the vegetables on a large, heated serving platter. Decorate with a couple of fresh flowers, and serve.

Photograph on page 231

Whole Wheat Rolls, Fresh Fruit, and Butter

(Makes 1½ dozen rolls)

Ingredients:
2 cups milk
1 package dry or ⅔ ounce compressed yeast
1 egg
2 tablespoons butter or margarine
¼ cup honey
1 teaspoon salt
½ cup corn meal
5½ cups whole wheat flour

Method:

1. Heat the milk to approximately 100 degrees or the temperature of a warm bath. Combine the milk with the yeast, egg, butter, honey, salt, and corn meal in a bowl. Let stand a few minutes to give the yeast a chance to grow.

2. Add the flour to make a soft and slightly sticky dough. The amount of flour to be added can vary depending upon the flour's ability to absorb liquid. It is advisable to add the last cup of flour slowly until a soft and slightly sticky dough is obtained.

3. Knead the dough by turning out onto a lightly floured worktable. Dust your hands with a little flour. Push your fingers into the dough and then press down with the heels of your hands, rolling the dough back and forth as you press. Keep kneading for approximately 5 minutes until the dough is elastic and satiny in texture.

4. Place the dough in a lightly oiled bowl, cover with a damp towel, and set aside in a warm place to rise.

5. When the dough doubles in bulk, deflate it by punching with your hand a few times. Divide the dough into 18 pieces. Roll each piece into a ball, and place on a nonstick or lightly oiled baking pan. Set pan in a warm place to rise.

6. When double in bulk, bake rolls until golden brown in a preheated 375 degree oven.

(Recipe continued on next page.)

(Serves 6)

Ingredients for fruit and butter:
¼ pound butter, softened
6 honeydew wedges
6 lime wedges
6 strawberries
6 whole wheat rolls, kept warm for serving (see recipe on previous page)

Method:

1. Using a pastry bag and a star tube, pipe out butter rosettes into small hors d'oeuvre cups, and refrigerate.

2. Place 1 wedge of honeydew with 1 wedge of lime onto each of 6 butter plates. With a sharp knife, cut thin slices into each strawberry without cutting through the stem end. Fan out the strawberries, and place 1 on each butter plate. Place a butter rosette onto the butter plates. Add the warm roll, and serve.

Photograph on page 226

Celery, Peas, and Smokehouse Almonds

(Serves 6)

Ingredients:
4 cups diced celery
1½ cups chicken stock or canned chicken consommé
2 cups frozen peas
⅓ cup Smokehouse almonds

Method:

1. In a covered saucepan, cook celery in chicken stock until tender but still crunchy. Add peas, toss, and heat.

2. Strain out liquid, place celery and peas on a platter, and garnish with almonds.

Photograph on page 221

Poppy's Rice Plate

---

five-grain rice with green beans, sliced apples, honey-roasted pecans, and currants

(Serves 6)

Ingredients:
½ cup long-grain brown rice
½ cup wild rice
½ cup barley
½ cup hard, red winter wheat
1 tablespoon sesame seeds
4 cups strongly flavored chicken stock or canned chicken consommé
¼ teaspoon whole saffron
1¼ pounds green beans
½ cup pecan halves
1 teaspoon honey
1 large apple
1 cup water
1 teaspoon lemon juice
1 tablespoon butter or margarine
salt and pepper, to taste
1½ tablespoons dried currants
6 radish roses (make perpendicular cuts to form petals around the outside of the radish, then place in cold water to open petals)
1 red bell pepper, cut into thin slices
1 yellow bell pepper, cut into thin slices

Method:

1. Combine the first five ingredients together. Rinse rice under cold water, and drain well. Place the mixture in a baking pan, and bake in a preheated 400 degree oven for 15 minutes to dry out mixture and brown slightly.

2. In the meantime, add the saffron to the chicken stock, and bring to a boil. Strain out the saffron. Add the liquid to the rice mixture in the baking pan, cover, and bake in a 400 degree oven for 1 hour.

3. Steam or boil the green beans until tender.

(Recipe continued on next page.)

4. Mix the pecans with the honey, place on a lightly oiled baking pan, and bake in a 400 degree oven for 10 minutes until lightly toasted.

5. Cut the apple into quarters, remove the core, and cut into ¼-inch-thick slices. Place in 1 cup of water mixed with 1 teaspoon of lemon juice to keep from browning.

6. To serve, scoop a portion of rice in the center of 6 dinner plates. Quickly sauté the green beans in the butter, add salt and pepper, and place around the mound of green beans. Place the apple slices, pecans, and currants on top of the green beans. Garnish each plate with a radish rose and red and yellow pepper slices.

Photograph on page 199

Sliced Green Beans with Toasted Almonds

(Serves 6)

Ingredients: 1½ pounds green beans, sliced
½ cup water
1 tablespoon butter or margarine
salt and black pepper, to taste
¼ cup toasted almonds (bake almonds in 400 degree oven for 10 minutes)

Method: 1. In a skillet with a tight-fitting lid, add the beans, water, and butter. Cover, and cook over high heat for a few minutes, then uncover, and continue to cook until all the water has evaporated and the beans are tender but still crunchy. This process should take approximately 4 to 5 minutes. Salt and pepper, and garnish with toasted almonds.

Photograph on page 168

Black Bean Chile

(Makes 2 quarts chile)

Ingredients:
1 cup chopped onion
⅔ cup chopped celery
⅔ cup chopped green bell pepper
2 tablespoons corn oil
2 tablespoons minced garlic
2 tablespoons minced Jalapeno pepper
1 pound black beans
2 quarts water
1 tablespoon salt
1 bay leaf
2 cups canned or fresh, chopped tomato with juice
2 tablespoons chopped cilantro or ground coriander
2 tablespoons chopped oregano
purple Kale or other decorative lettuce leaves

Method:

1. In a large, heavy metal pot, sauté the onions, celery, and bell peppers in oil until some browning occurs on the edges of the vegetables. Add the garlic and Jalapeno peppers. Sauté for 1 minute. Add the beans, water, salt, bay leaf, and tomatoes. Cook on a low flame, stirring from time to time until the beans are tender and the mixture has thickened.

2. Remove the chile from the burner. Mix in the cilantro and oregano. Place mixture in the center of a large serving platter, and garnish with decorative lettuce leaves.

Photograph on page 194

Carrots and Broccoli with Soy and Sesame Seed Dressing

(Serves 6)

Ingredients:
1½ pounds broccoli

1½ pounds carrots

2 tablespoons light sesame seed oil or peanut oil

6 green onion curls (trim the green onions to 3-inches in length, then cut along the length of the green portion, leaving the bulb intact, and place in cold water to curl)

Method:

1. Wash broccoli, and discard the coarse leaves and lower part of the stalks. Halve or quarter the bunches lengthwise, depending on their size, to make them all no more than ½-inch in diameter at the base. Steam or boil until the broccoli is tender but still crunchy.

2. Peel, and grate the carrots using the finest attachment of a rotary grater. (Rotary graters can be purchased at most gourmet shops and restaurant supply stores.) In a large skillet over high heat, sauté the grated carrot in the oil until a large portion of the carrots become browned and crunchy.

3. To serve, mound the carrots in the center of a serving platter, and place the broccoli and green onion curls around the sides. Serve with Soy and Sesame Seed Dressing on the side (recipe on page 43).

Photograph on page 222

Magic Wands

(Makes 2 dozen magic wands)

Ingredients:
1¼ cups water
1 package dry yeast
2½ tablespoons brown sugar
1½ teaspoons salt
⅓ cup corn meal
1¾ cup unbleached, all-purpose flour
1¾ cup whole wheat flour
1 egg, beaten
sesame seeds

Method:

1. Preheat oven to 400 degrees.

2. Heat the water to approximately 100 degrees or the temperature of a warm bath. Dissolve the yeast, sugar, and salt into the water in a mixing bowl.

3. Add the corn meal and flour until a fairly stiff dough is formed. Turn dough onto a lightly floured board and knead until smooth and satiny.

4. Roll out 24 8-inch strips of dough approximately ½-inch in thickness to form the staffs of the wands. Place on a lightly oiled or nonstick baking pan.

5. Roll out the remaining dough with a rolling pin. Cut out stars using a small star cookie cutter. Brush the staffs with a beaten egg, and attach a star to one end of each staff. Brush the stars with the egg, and sprinkle with sesame seeds.

6. Set the pan in a warm area, and let the wands rise until double in bulk.

7. Bake 12 to 15 minutes until golden brown.

Serving Suggestion: Serve the wands warm with Cinderella Salad (recipe on page 40) and your choice of Salad Dressing (recipes on pages 42-44). Just for fun, pass out directional cards to your guests explaining how to use the magic wands. Make up your own directions or feel free to use mine (see next page).

(Recipe continued on next page.)

* * * * * * * *

How To Use Your Magic Wand

1. *For Health and Happiness — Wave Up and Down*

2. *For Peace and Contentment — Wave From Left to Right*

3. *To Lose Weight Quickly — Keep Waving Wand*

* * * * * * * *

Photograph on page 163

Mama Es' Noodle Pudding

(Serves 8 to 10)

Ingredients:
1 pound noodles, cooked
4 eggs
1 cup sugar
1½ cups cottage cheese
½ cup dark raisins
2 cups sour cream
¼ cup strawberry jelly
2 teaspoons cinnamon
2 teaspoons pure vanilla extract
¼ cup butter or margarine, melted

> **Who Is Mama Es?**
>
> *For information concerning Mama Es, please send a self-addressed, stamped envelope to:*
> *Mama Es*
> *Golden's Kitchen*
> *2811 E. Calaveros Dr.*
> *Phoenix, AZ 85028*

Method:

1. Mix all of the ingredients together excluding the butter.

2. Spread the melted butter on the bottom and along the sides of a 16-inch by 11-inch baking pan. Place the noodle mixture inside the pan, and bake in a preheated 400 degree oven for approximately 1 hour until the noodles are crisp and golden brown on top.

Photograph on page 200

Snake Bread

(Serves 8)

Ingredients:
2 cups water
2 packages dry yeast
1 teaspoon anise seed
⅓ cup honey
1 tablespoon salt
1 tablespoon vegetable oil
3 cups unbleached, all-purpose flour
3 cups whole wheat flour
1 egg, beaten with 2 tablespoons water
sesame seeds
poppy seeds
red food coloring paste (food coloring paste, which I prefer to liquid food
   coloring, can be purchased in cake decorating and restaurant
   supply stores)
2 raisins

Method:

1. Heat the water to approximately 100 degrees or the temperature of a warm bath. Combine the water, yeast, anise seed, honey, salt, and vegetable oil in a bowl. Let the mixture stand for approximately 15 minutes to give the yeast a chance to grow.

2. Add the flour to make a soft and slightly sticky dough. Knead the dough for approximately 5 minutes until it is elastic and satiny in texture.

3. Place the dough in a lightly oiled bowl, cover with a damp towel or plastic wrap, and set the bowl in a warm area for approximately 30 minutes until it is double in bulk. Deflate by punching it with your hand a few times.

4. Remove a small piece of dough to make the snake's tongue and set aside. Roll out the remaining dough until it is approximately 5 feet in length, tapering the dough at one end to form the body of the snake. Brush the dough with the beaten egg and water, and sprinkle alternately with sesame seeds and poppy seeds leaving the area for the snake's head seedless. Curl the dough up into a coiled snake position, and place it on a lightly oiled or nonstick baking pan.

(Recipe continued on next page.)

5. Color the reserved dough red, and roll it out to the thickness of a toothpick. Cut it almost all the way in half to form a snake's forked tongue. Attach the tongue to the head by making a hole with a toothpick where the snake's mouth should be. Then insert the tongue into the hole. Push the 2 raisins into the head to form its eyes.

6. Place the snake in a warm area, and let it rise until double in bulk. Then bake in a preheated 350 degree oven for approximately 50 minutes.

Photograph on page 201

Lima Beans and Yellow Summer Squash

(Serves 6)

Ingredients:
4 cups lima beans, fresh or frozen
1 cup water
1 tablespoon butter or margarine
2 yellow squash, cut into thin, half-moon pieces
¼ cup julienne red bell pepper
¼ cup cut chives

Method:

1. In a skillet over high heat, cook lima beans in water and butter until the beans are tender and the water is completely evaporated.

2. Toss in the yellow squash. Stir, and cook for 1 minute.

3. Roll out mixture on a warm serving platter, and garnish with bell peppers and chives.

Photograph on page 220

Mixed Grilled Vegetables with Fresh Water Chestnuts

This recipe calls for using fresh water chestnuts that can be purchased
in many supermarkets and Oriental produce stores.

The difference between fresh water chestnuts and their canned or frozen counterpart
is the difference between day and night.

Fresh water chestnuts are crunchy and have a fresh, sweet, coconut flavor.
Canned or frozen water chestnuts are still crunchy, but have no flavor at all.

(Serves 6)

Ingredients:
12 small carrots, peeled
1 large zucchini, cut into half-moons, 1-inch in thickness
1 purple onion, cut into 12 wedges
2 red bell peppers, cut into 2-inch by 1-inch pieces
¼ pound Chinese snow peas
2 tablespoons light sesame seed oil or peanut oil
1½ cups fresh, peeled water chestnuts

Method:

1. Steam, boil, or microwave carrots until they are tender but still crunchy.

2. Mix all of the vegetables together with the oil. Cook over a preheated charcoal broiler or under a preheated oven broiler until the vegetables are tender and have some browning. Add the water chestnuts, heat for a few seconds, then serve.

Photograph on page 192

The Curried Tuna Catastrophe

The next time you try a new recipe only to watch your diners push their forks around their plates searching for something to eat, feel free to refer to this little story. It may make you feel better.

One day, many years ago, I woke up at 5:30 on a July morning feeling peppy and primed. While putting on two pairs of white cotton socks and working shoes with heavy soles, I looked forward to serving a new lunch at camp Na-Sho-Pa, a co-ed overnight children's summer camp that had the best camp swimming pool I have ever seen ... and the worst kitchen.

The first to arrive on the kitchen scene, I didn't have to unlock the doors. Some hungry campers had done the honors for me during a midnight kitchen raid. Short of an electric, barbed wire fence, nothing would have stopped the "night-raiders" from slipping into the kitchen — the most ingenious and daring activity in camp, and no doubt, the most fulfilling. During my twelve-year tenure as chef, I became accustomed to these raids and the mousy scraps of food they left on the floor. Without hesitation, I took out the dust pan and broom, swept up the tuna fish and corn flakes, then proceeded, as usual, to light the ovens, turn on the exhaust fans, and put up an urn of coffee.

When the entire kitchen crew arrived, we went over the menu, and discussed my new lunch creation — curried tuna fish on toasted English muffin with melted Swiss cheese. Mind you, the Swiss cheese was not your domestic brand that comes individually wrapped and pre-sliced. I decided to splurge with an imported, aged cheese that had flavor.

You're probably saying, "Kids don't eat that." You see, years ago, I was in college studying "gourmet cooking." Today, I realize that a juicy charcoal-broiled hamburger on a freshly baked bun can be just as "gourmet" as Beef Wellington. But at that time, I was frustrated, and wanted to cook anything with a new seasoning, something with wine, something a little more unusual than fish sticks and mashed potatoes. In my mind, I envisioned the kids devouring my new creation. They loved tuna fish. After all, I'd just finished sweeping up the tuna left from the "night-raiders." They also enjoyed toasted English muffins for breakfast. I paid little attention to the fact that the average American child eats American cheese, not imported, aged Swiss, and that curry powder is as foreign to most kids as a Hostess Twinkie is to a wild gorilla. I knew that when cooking for kids, it's wise to keep in mind what the average mother would prepare for her children: something simple, not Lobster Newburg, not a lot of exotic seasonings, mushrooms, and cut up vegetables. But that day in July, for my own sanity and to expose the kids to something new and unusual, I had to serve my curried tuna entrée.

(The Curried Tuna Catastrophe continued on next page.)

It wasn't easy preparing the new recipe for six hundred people. I cooked samples for the kitchen staff, and we decided two of the open-faced sandwiches would be plenty for each camper. We began by toasting twelve hundred muffins in five hundred and fifty degree ovens while a hundred and fifty pounds of curried tuna salad was being prepared in the pantry. In the middle of a summer heat wave, the ovens at full blast brought temperatures in the compact kitchen — originally designed to feed two hundred people — to one hundred and fifty degrees. The cooks wore headbands and drank plenty of water as we scooped the prepared tuna onto the toasted English muffins, placed freshly sliced cheese on top, and set the sheet pans holding the creation aside until serving time.

As the campers came marching into the dining room, we slipped the sheet pans into the ovens to melt the cheese. Waiters quickly served a salad and came back into the kitchen to pick up the "piece de resistance." They looked good. The English muffins were nicely toasted. The cheese, shiny and stringy with a little browning, topped the majestic golden yellow, curried tuna. As the first large stainless steel platters were passed around the dining room tables, I hoped that twelve hundred curried tuna muffins would be ample for the hungry campers.

Then, the first sign of trouble. The first waiter on line, who served the fifteen-year-old girls, returned with the entire platter still full. They're on a diet again, I told myself. All they're going to eat for lunch is salad. But, a few moments later, panic struck as each platter came back to the kitchen full of my delicious curried tuna on toasted English muffins with perfectly melted imported, aged Swiss cheese. One of the cooks shouted the battle cry: "Get out the peanut butter and jelly!"

Within five minutes, twenty-six waiters were scrambling in a kitchen no larger than the size of an average living room. They were looking for something to feed the impoverished patrons. In the pantry, tuna fish salad was quickly being prepared with just mayonnaise: no seasoning, no vegetables. The previous day's leftover food came out of the refrigerators while stores of peanut butter, jelly, plain tuna and American cheese were rapidly being depleted. One of the waiters tripped over a platter of curried tuna muffins that had accidentally fallen to the ground. Counselors ran into the kitchen to find out what kind of trick I was playing on them, and the campers began to chant, "We want food. We want food." Louder and louder they cried until the sound echoed off the tin roof, and everyone in the kitchen had to shout to be heard. It was pandemonium — the food service equivalent of Custer's last stand.

Before we go on with the story, let's take a moment to reflect on the eating habits of children: Most people would say cooking for kids is no big deal. After all, they are not like adults who have developed a sophisticated, discerning palate. Give them hamburgers, hot dogs, and french fries and they'll be happy. The question is, how do they develop into adults with sophisticated, discerning palates when their food sources are limited to three items on the menu? Another difference is that if we, as adults, come across a new dish we do not particularly care for, depending on the situation, we either politely request a substitute or leave the food on the plate with the excuse that we are not terribly hungry. Not kids — they are much too honest. Instead, their first response will be: "Yuck! What is that?" Informed the dish before them is curried tuna fish on English muffin with melted Swiss cheese, the next response will be: "It's whaaaat?" And the final response: "I'm starving. May I please have something to *eat*?"

(The Curried Tuna Catastrophe continued on next page.)

Therefore, to cook for children with the intention of educating their little palates, one runs the risk of castigation and guilt, often followed by severe depression.

To say the curried tuna sandwiches bombed would be an understatement. To me, a meal is a bomb when half of the people refrain from eating the dish. It seemed to me that more curried tuna fish sandwiches came back into the kitchen than we sent out. To make matters worse, we did not have enough peanut butter and jelly, plain tuna, leftovers, and other food substitutes. According to the camp mothers, the children were still hungry. Hungry! Innocent children were still hungry, and I was responsible.

The campers slowly filed out through the dining room doors. The kitchen crew stood still. Sweating profusely, we stared at one another in silence. There was nothing to say, and we needed strength to clean up the mess. I felt castigated and guilty. I was depressed, but not severely — because in the back of my mind, I was looking forward to serving a new dessert for dinner — chocolate cake made with whipped cream and M&M's — a guaranteed winner!

Proper food etiquette is an integral part

of civilized society.

But when there are no established rules,

or when the rules cannot apply to your particular situation —

do what you think is best,

then relax and enjoy the pleasures

of good food and company.

Fruits, Eggs

and

Cheeses

Eggs Albert

poached eggs with sherry sauce, asparagus, and toast triangles

(Serves 6)

Ingredients:
36 large, green asparagus spears
6 eggs
4 cups whole or 2% milk
1 bay leaf
⅓ cup unbleached, all-purpose flour
½ cup dry sherry
1½ teaspoons salt
¼ teaspoon cayenne pepper
whole wheat or rye bread
chervil or parsley

Method:

1. Peel the asparagus stalks, and remove the ends that are tough. Cook the asparagus in salted, boiling water until they are tender, then cool immediately in cold water to keep them green. Cut each asparagus spear approximately 2 inches below the tip. Reserve the tips, and cut the asparagus bottoms into ½-inch pieces.

2. Poach the eggs in simmering water for approximately 2½ minutes. Drain on a towel and trim the ragged edges from around each poached egg.

3. In a saucepan, mix the milk, bay leaf, and flour. Cook over a medium-high heat, continuously stirring, until the mixture comes to a boil and thickens. Lower the heat, add sherry, salt, and cayenne pepper. Let the sauce simmer for approximately 15 minutes, stirring from time to time.

4. Cut 48 2-inch-long triangles from whole wheat or rye bread. Toast in a preheated 500 degree oven for 6 to 8 minutes.

5. To serve, place one poached egg onto each of the 6 dinner plates. Spoon the sauce over the eggs. Place 6 asparagus tips on each plate along with some of the cut asparagus. Sprinkle top of sauce with a little cayenne pepper and some chopped chervil. Place a sprig of chervil on top of the eggs, and line the outside of each plate with 8 toast triangles.

Photograph on page 170

Kiwi Fruit, Mangoes, and Berries

(Serves 6)

Ingredients: 3 kiwi fruit
2 mangoes
1 pint raspberries
1 pint blackberries
2 sprigs mint

Method:
1. With a sharp paring knife, peel and slice the kiwi fruit and mangoes.

2. Place the berries in the center of a serving platter with the mangoes and kiwi fruit on the outside, and garnish with the mint sprigs.

Photograph on page 226

Sliced Fruit

While watching a blackjack dealer fan out a new deck on the table, each card equidistant, I was inspired to do the same. Instead of cards, I used fruit.

Ingredients: just about any fruit
mint leaves to garnish
cranberry juice

Method:
1. With a sharp knife, cut fruit into uniform slices, and lay out on serving plates in a pattern of your choice. For a pretty color, pour some cranberry juice in the center of the plate.

Photographs on pages 228 & 229

Green Onion and Mushroom Quesadilla

green onion, olive, and mushroom quesadilla with southwest salsa

(Makes 6 quesadillas)

Ingredients:
6 8-inch flour tortillas
1 pound mild, yellow Cheddar cheese, grated
1 pound white Jack cheese, grated
½ cup chopped, green onion
12 pitted, black olives, cut into slivers
12 large mushrooms, sliced

Method:
1. Preheat oven to 400 degrees.

2. Lay out flour tortillas on sheet pans. Portion out cheese, onions, olives, and mushrooms on each tortilla. At this point, the quesadillas can be prepared ahead of time, covered with plastic wrap, and refrigerated.

3. Ten minutes before serving, place prepared quesadillas in the oven for 7 to 10 minutes until the cheese has completely melted and there is some browning around the edges of the tortillas. Serve Southwest Salsa on the side (see next recipe).

Photograph on page 205

Southwest Salsa

(Makes 2½ cups salsa)

Ingredients:
2 cups tomatoes, peeled and chopped (to peel tomatoes, place in boiling water for 10 seconds, let cool, then remove peel with a paring knife)
¼ cup chopped chile peppers
2 tablespoons chopped cilantro

(Recipe continued on next page.)

Ingredients continued:

2 tablespoons red wine vinegar
1 teaspoon salt
½ teaspoon granulated sugar
½ teaspoon minced garlic
1 jalapeno pepper, minced

Method:

1. Mix all of the ingredients together.

Photograph on page 205

Cranapple-Blueberry Yogurt Parfait

(Serves 6)

Ingredients:

6 apples, peeled and chopped
1 cup cranberries, fresh or frozen
1 pint apple juice
1½ cups plain 2% yogurt mixed with 1 tablespoon light-brown sugar
1½ cups blueberries
6 strawberry slices
6 sprigs mint

Method:

1. In a saucepan, cook apples and cranberries over medium heat until the apples are tender and the liquid has been reduced to form a chunky, applesauce-like consistency. Refrigerate until chilled.

2. Place a scoop of cranapple sauce into each of 6 wine or parfait glasses. Spoon ¼ cup of yogurt, and then ¼ cup of blueberries on top of the cranapple sauce. Garnish with a slice of strawberry and a sprig of mint.

Photograph on page 167

Scrambled Eggs with Chile Peppers and Cheese

(Serves 6)

Ingredients: ½ pound Jack cheese, sliced ¼-inch in thickness
½ pound Cheddar cheese, sliced ¼-inch in thickness
1 tablespoon butter or margarine
½ cup finely diced chile peppers
1 teaspoon minced garlic
12 eggs
2 tablespoons milk
2 teaspoons chopped cilantro or parsley
4 thin slices red bell pepper
3 whole chives

Method:

1. Cut triangular shapes of cheese. Place on a large serving platter to form an interesting design. Set the platter in a low oven, approximately 200 degrees, for a few minutes to melt the cheese. While the cheese is melting, cook the eggs.

2. On a medium burner, heat the butter in a large skillet. Add the chile peppers. Stir, and cook for a few minutes until peppers are tender. Add the garlic and cook approximately 30 seconds. Beat the eggs and milk in a bowl, and add them to the chile peppers and garlic. Stir, and cook the eggs until they are no longer raw, but still soft, shiny, and moist.

3. Place the scrambled eggs in the center of the platter on top of the melted cheese. Sprinkle eggs with chopped cilantro, and garnish with red pepper and chives.

Photograph on page 215

Ruth's Fruit

This dish can be served as a dessert or a cold soup.

(Serves 6)

Ingredients:
1½ cups apple juice
1½ cups orange juice
1½ cups diced honeydew melon
1½ cups raspberries
1½ cups cut papaya or mango or peaches
1 cup canned gooseberries with juice from the can
1 cup blueberries
1 cup seedless grapes
1 small lime, cut into very thin slices
¾ cup egg whites
1½ tablespoons granulated sugar

Method:
1. In a blender, purée the apple juice and orange juice with ½ cup honeydew melon, ½ cup raspberries, and ½ cup papaya. Pour the thickened juice mixture into a bowl and add the remaining fruit. Chill well.

2. Before serving, beat the egg whites in a whipping bowl with the sugar until soft peaks are formed. Place fruit mixture on a large serving platter or individual serving dishes. Garnish with a dollop of meringue.

Photograph on page 189

The New-Fashioned Fruit Plate

(Serves 6)

Ingredients:
1½ cups plain 2% yogurt
1 tablespoon granulated sugar
¼ teaspoon pure vanilla extract
6 slices dried date, cut into ¼-inch rounds
1 cup Ricotta cheese
1 cup lowfat cottage cheese
3 tablespoons drained, canned, crushed pineapple
1 pint raspberries
6 bunches green grapes
1½ papayas, peeled, seeded, cut into quarters, and sliced
6 whole strawberries
6 sprigs mint

Method:

1. Mix the yogurt, sugar, and vanilla together. Portion out ¼ cup of this mixture onto 6 7-inch luncheon plates. Tip and rotate the plates until the yogurt mixture is evenly distributed within the borders of the plates.

2. Place a piece of date off-center on each plate (a little hidden surprise). Mix the Ricotta cheese, cottage cheese, and crushed pineapple together. Scoop a ⅓ cup portion of cottage cheese mixture over each date.

3. Purée ⅓ cup of raspberries through a fine sieve. Using a pastry bag and a thin pastry tube for writing, pipe out two lines of raspberry purée on top of the yogurt. With the point of a knife, make perpendicular zig-zags through the raspberry purée.

4. Line the cottage cheese mixture with the remaining raspberries. Place the green grapes and sliced papaya on each side, top it off with a strawberry, and garnish with a mint sprig. Cover each finished plate with plastic wrap, and refrigerate until serving time.

5. Serve with Cinnamon Toast (recipe on page 124).

Photograph on page 166

The Old-Fashioned Fruit Plate

(Serves 6)

Ingredients: 2 heads Boston or green leaf lettuce leaves
1½ cups Ricotta cheese
1½ cups lowfat cottage cheese
¼ cup drained, canned, crushed pineapple
assorted fresh fruit (grapes, strawberries, oranges, papaya, blueberries,
   raspberries, melon, kiwi fruit, etc.)
mint sprigs

Method:

1. Line 6 9- or 10-inch dinner plates with the lettuce leaves.

2. Mix the Ricotta cheese, cottage cheese, and crushed pineapple together. Scoop a ½ cup portion of cottage cheese mixture into the center of each plate. Place assorted fresh fruit around the cottage cheese, and garnish with a few mint sprigs.

3. Cover each finished plate with plastic wrap, and refrigerate until serving time.

4. Serve with Cream Cheese-Raisin Finger Sandwiches (recipe on page 124).

Photograph on page 166

Cinnamon Toast

(Serves 6)

Ingredients: 9 pieces whole wheat bread
melted butter or margarine
2 tablespoons granulated sugar mixed with 1 teaspoon cinnamon

Method:
1. Cut bread slices on the diagonal to form 18 bread triangles. Lay out bread on a baking sheet, brush with melted butter, and sprinkle with cinnamon-sugar mixture.

2. Bake in a preheated, 500 degree oven for 8 to 10 minutes. Serve the toast warm.

Photograph on page 166

Cream Cheese-Raisin Finger Sandwiches

(Serves 6)

Ingredients: 8 slices raisin bread
8 ounces cream cheese

Method:
1. Lay out 4 slices of bread, spread with cream cheese, and cover with remaining 4 slices of bread. With a sharp knife, trim off crust from sandwiches, and cut each sandwich into 3 equal rectangular pieces.

2. Serve 2 finger sandwiches per person, preferably at room temperature, on bread and butter plates.

Photograph on page 166

Baked Apples

Just as it is important to choose the right potato for baking, it is equally important
to choose the best variety of apple for baking.

The most popular apple, the Red Delicious, is delicious eaten raw;
but when baked, it falls apart.

My favorite for baking is the Winesap; next in preference are the
Newtown Pippin, Granny Smith, and Rome Beauty.

(Serves 6)

Ingredients:
6 apples, suitable for baking
3 teaspoons light brown sugar
1 pint unfiltered apple juice
ground cinnamon
6 fresh flowers
6 sprigs mint

Method:

1. Preheat oven to 375 degrees.

2. Cut off the stem portion of the apples, and scoop out the apple core with a melon baller, making sure not to scoop through the bottom of the apples.

3. Place the apples in a baking dish. Portion out ½ teaspoon of brown sugar into the center of each apple. Pour the apple juice over the apples, and in the bottom of the baking pan. Lightly sprinkle the tops of the apples with the ground cinnamon.

4. Bake for approximately 1 hour and 15 minutes until the apples are soft but not broken.

5. To serve, pour 2 tablespoons of juice from the baking dish over each apple. Garnish with a fresh flower and a mint sprig.

Photograph on page 176

Holiday Fruit Platter

(Serves 6)

Ingredients:
2 tangerines
3 pears
4 crab apples
6 small bunches grapes
6 dates
1 pint strawberries
orange leaves (if available)
spray bottle of water

Method:

1. Arrange the fruit on a large serving platter, and garnish with the orange leaves.

2. Before serving, spray fruit with water.

Photograph on page 169

Nectarines with Prunes

(Serves 6)

Ingredients: 1½ pounds nectarines
12 dried prunes
¼ cup honey
¼ cup water

Method:
1. Cut each nectarine in half around the pit. Holding the nectarines in the palms of your hands, gently rotate the cut nectarine, each half in the opposite direction. This will help the nectarine come lose from the pit on one side. With a paring knife, gently pry the pit away from the attached nectarine half. Cut the pitless halves into quarters, and lay out on a serving tray. Add the dried prunes to the platter.

2. Mix the honey and water together in a spray bottle. Spray a mist of honey water onto the prepared platter of fruit, and serve.

Photograph on page 204

Dutch Apple Yogurt

(Makes 1 quart yogurt)

Ingredients: 6 medium-sized apples (preferably Granny Smith), peeled and sliced
1 pint apple juice
1 pint plain 2% yogurt
1 teaspoon ground cinnamon
¼ cup dark raisins
garnish — raspberries, currants, and a mint sprig

Method:
1. In a saucepan over high heat, cook the apples in apple juice until they are tender and the liquid is reduced to form a chunky, applesauce consistency. Remove from the burner, and let the mixture cool.

2. Add remaining ingredients. Mix.

3. Pour into individual serving dishes. Garnish with raspberries, currants, and a mint sprig.

Photograph on page 209

Long-Stemmed Strawberries with Honey Water

(Serves 6)

Ingredients: 14 California long-stemmed strawberries
parsley sprigs
¼ cup honey
¼ cup water

Method:

1. Wipe the strawberries clean with a damp towel. Lay out 12 strawberries on a large oval platter in 2 rows, criss-crossing their stems.

2. Remove the long stems from the remaining 2 berries. Slice them without cutting through the stem portion. Fan out the strawberries, and place them on the sides of the platter, stem down. Garnish the platter with the sprigs of parsley.

3. Mix the honey and water together in a spray bottle. Spray a mist of honey water onto the prepared platter of strawberries, and serve.

Photograph on page 172

Remember:

KIN CAYW

Keep It Neat and Clean As You Work.

also

A small taste while cooking and before serving

is a cook's guarantee of quality.

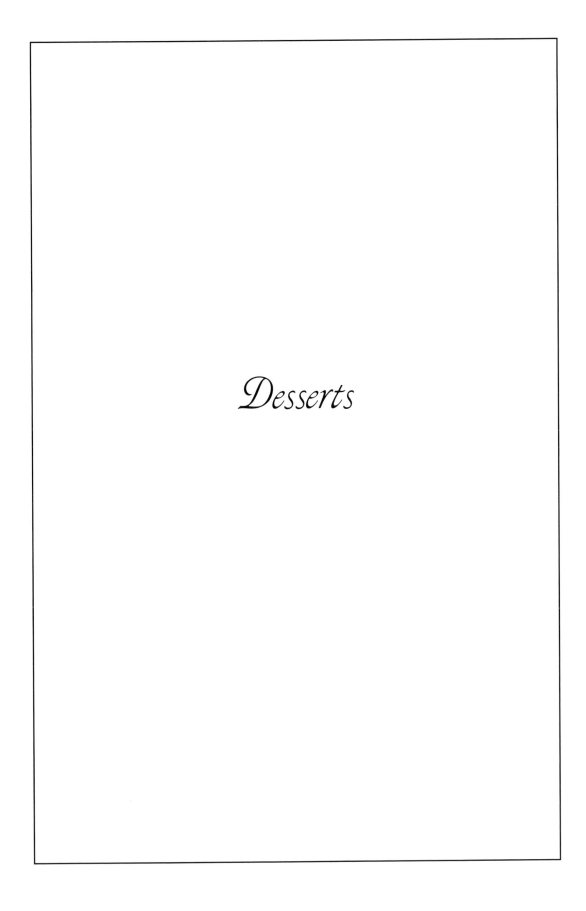

Desserts

Eating moderately

is often more difficult

than abstinence.

But, it is a lot more fun!

Super Chocolate Chip Cookies

What makes these cookies attain "super" status is the amount and quality of chocolate used.

This recipe calls for two to three times the usual amount and
uses the finest quality chocolate cut into chips.

(Makes 5 dozen cookies)

Ingredients:
1½ cups unbleached, all-purpose flour
1½ cups whole wheat flour
½ tablespoon baking soda
1½ teaspoons salt
¾ pound butter
1 cup granulated sugar
1 cup brown sugar
3 eggs
½ tablespoon pure vanilla extract
1½ pounds of a fine quality bittersweet chocolate, chopped into pieces (I use Callebaut, imported from Belgium.)
3 cups toasted, slivered almonds (bake almonds in 400 degree oven for 10 minutes)

Method:
1. Preheat oven to 375 degrees.

2. Using a sieve, sift the flours, baking soda, and salt together. There will be some bran left in the sieve from the whole wheat flour. Discard it or use it for your breakfast cereal, but it is best to leave it out of this recipe.

3. In a mixing bowl, cream the butter and sugars together. Beat in the eggs one at a time. Add the vanilla. Mix in the flour. Stir in the chocolate and nuts.

4. Using a #60 scoop, portion out dough onto a nonstick or lightly buttered baking pan. Bake approximately 12 minutes.

Photograph on page 223

Diamonds on Coffee Ice Cream

(Serves approximately 20 people)

Ingredients: 3 quarts coffee ice cream

1 package Nabisco chocolate wafers or other thin chocolate cookies

7 ounces almond paste (can be purchased in most supermarkets and gourmet stores)

pink and green food coloring paste (food coloring paste, which I prefer to liquid food coloring, can be purchased in cake decorating and restaurant supply stores)

1 cup heavy cream

3 tablespoons light brown sugar

1 teaspoon finely ground, instant coffee (coffee can be finely ground with a rolling pin)

Method:

1. Soften ice cream at room temperature for a little while, but don't let it melt.

2. Pack a quart of ice cream in the bottom of a 12-inch round cake pan. Place a layer of chocolate wafers on top. Pack another quart of ice cream, and then another layer of wafers. Pack in the final quart of ice cream. Set the cake pan in the freezer for at least 3 hours.

3. When the ice cream is firm, unmold the ice cream onto a serving platter by placing the outside of the cake pan in a warm bath of water for approximately 30 seconds. Place the serving platter on top of the ice cream, and flip the cake pan over so that the ice cream slides onto the platter. With a spatula, smooth out the top and sides of the ice cream. Clean the platter with a warm, wet towel, then place it back into the freezer for the ice cream to firm up.

4. In the meantime, color half of the almond paste with pink food coloring and the other half with green food coloring. Roll out the almond paste between 2 pieces of wax paper until it is ¼-inch in thickness. With a sharp paring knife or an X-acto knife, cut 24 small diamonds for the border. Cut out 9 large diamonds for the center, along with 9 smaller ones that will go on top of the large diamonds. Roll out almond paste balls to go on top of each diamond.

(Recipe continued on next page.)

5. In a chilled bowl, beat the heavy cream, brown sugar, and coffee together until stiff peaks are formed. Using a pastry bag and a star tube, pipe out 24 rosettes along the border of the ice cream mold and top each with a small diamond and a ball. Place the large diamonds in the center of the ice cream, then pipe small rosettes around the diamonds filling in the center portion of the ice cream. When completely decorated, set the ice cream cake back into the freezer to firm before serving. This cake can be made days in advance, and kept in a large plastic bag in the freezer.

Photograph on page 209

White Chocolate-Graham Cracker Clusters

(Makes approximately 2 dozen clusters)

Ingredients: 1½ pounds white chocolate (I use Callebaut, imported from Belgium.)
⅔ pound or 2 packages Nabisco honey graham crackers
½ cup white raisins

Method:

1. Melt the chocolate in a 150 degree oven or over a double boiler.

2. Chop graham crackers into 1-inch-size pieces, and fold them with the raisins into the melted chocolate.

3. Spoon out on wax paper, and refrigerate until the clusters have hardened.

Photograph on page 207

3/14/86

We respectfully
request chocolate
souffle for dinner
tomorrow night.

Mr. McCann
Marcelle Rosen

Rae Willie   Jerome Dresser
                              Joan Crabtree
Margaret Hayhurst   Ginger Mayer
Lee Theis   Sally O'Brien
Ann Beale   Lulee Espy
Joyce Gutman   Anne Leintaly
Phyllis Kinder   Mildred Ragoffi
Barbara Franke   Nettie Jone
Susanah Mead   Ann Claycomb
Nell Revel   Rosemary Brown
                              Estoline Sherman
Mary Clare Broadbent
Marjorie Watkins
Dottee Walsh
Anita Lutz

Saturday Night's Chocolate Soufflé

(Serves 6)

Ingredients: ⅓ cup unbleached, all-purpose flour

⅓ cup granulated sugar

1½ cups milk

8 ounces of a fine quality bittersweet chocolate, chopped into small pieces

⅓ cup Kahlua or other coffee-flavored liqueur

1 tablespoon pure vanilla extract

¼ teaspoon salt

8 egg yolks

11 egg whites

¼ teaspoon cream of tartar

2 tablespoons granulated sugar

Method:

1. Prepare an 8-cup soufflé bowl by lightly buttering and sprinkling granulated sugar inside the bowl. Wrap a sheet of buttered aluminum foil around the outside of the bowl. Staple its ends together to form a collar around the bowl.

2. In a saucepan, add the flour, ⅓ cup sugar, and milk. Heat, and stir until mixture comes to a boil and thickens.

3. Remove from heat, add the chocolate, Kahlua, vanilla, and salt. Stir in the egg yolks. This part of the soufflé may be made in advance, set aside for a few hours, or refrigerated overnight. If you refrigerate the mixture, reheat slowly to room temperature.

4. About two hours before you plan to serve the soufflé, preheat oven to 375 degrees.

5. In a mixing bowl, beat the egg whites until they foam. Add the cream of tartar and 2 tablespoons of sugar. Continue to beat until stiff peaks just begin to form.

(Recipe continued on next page.)

6. Gently fold the egg whites into the chocolate mixture until the last trace of egg whites disappears. Pour the mixture into the prepared soufflé bowl. Place the soufflé bowl in a pan filled with water to a depth of 1 inch. Bake in a 375 degree oven for 1½ hours. Serve with Soufflé Sauce on the side (see next recipe).

Photograph on page 206

Soufflé Sauce

(Makes 3 cups soufflé sauce)

Ingredients:
1 cup heavy cream
2 tablespoons brown sugar
2 tablespoons Kahlua
1 teaspoon pure vanilla extract
¼ cup 2% milk
chocolate shavings

Method:

1. Place the cream, sugar, Kahlua, and vanilla extract in a chilled whipping bowl. Beat until mixture thickens and forms stiff peaks. Mix in the milk.

2. Pour into a chilled serving bowl, and sprinkle with chocolate shavings.

Photograph on page 206

Special Cookie

a chocolate chip cookie decorated with whipped cream, marzipan balls, and a candle

(Serves 1)

Ingredients: 1 chocolate chip cookie (recipe on page 133)
½ cup heavy cream
1½ tablespoons brown sugar
1 tablespoon Kahlua or Creme de Menthe or other favorite liqueur
almond paste (can be purchased in most supermarkets and gourmet stores)
assorted food coloring pastes (food coloring paste, which I prefer to liquid food coloring, can be purchased in cake decorating and restaurant supply stores)
1 candle

Method:
1. Place the cookie in the center of a dinner plate.

2. In a chilled mixing bowl, beat the heavy cream, brown sugar, and liqueur together until stiff peaks are formed. Using a pastry bag with a star tube, pipe out a pattern of rosettes on top and around the cookie.

3. Mix the almond paste with assorted food colors and roll into little balls. Place the balls in the centers of the whipped cream rosettes.

4. Place a candle in the center, light it, and let your guest of honor make a wish before he or she blows out the candle. If the wish is for another cookie, see steps 1 through 3, and then serve. Make sure to omit step 4 — 2 cookies and all that whipped cream is enough special treat for any special person!

Photograph on page 190

Baklava

This modified, easy-to-make rendition of traditional Baklava
uses no butter nor oils in its preparation.

Because of the high oil content in nuts, perhaps Baklava
should have always been made this way. Be the judge.

(Makes 12 pieces Baklava)

Ingredients: ½ cup chopped pecans
½ cup chopped, unsalted pistachio nuts
½ cup sesame seeds
¼ cup honey
1¼ teaspoons lemon juice
1¼ teaspoons cinnamon
12 5-inch by 5-inch sheets fillo dough
½ cup orange juice
½ cup apple juice
½ cup honey
3 apples, peeled, cored, and each cut into 6 wedges
confectioners sugar
cinnamon
a few mint sprigs

Method: 1. Preheat oven to 400 degrees.

2. Mix the first 6 ingredients together. Portion out a tablespoon of mixture
into the center of each sheet of fillo dough. Bring the corners of the
dough together, and pinch above the nut mixture. Place on a lightly
oiled or nonstick sheet pan. Bake for approximately 10 minutes until
golden brown. Set aside until serving time.

3. Mix the orange juice, apple juice, and honey in a saucepan. Add the
apple wedges, and cook until the apples are tender.

4. To serve, warm Baklava in the oven for a minute or two. Pour the juice
and apples on a serving platter. Sprinkle the Baklava with confectioners
sugar and cinnamon. Place on the platter and decorate with a few
sprigs of mint.

Photograph on page 224

Strawberry Shortcake

(Serves 6)

Ingredients:
2 cups and 3 tablespoons unbleached, all-purpose flour
2 teaspoons baking powder
½ teaspoon salt
pinch of nutmeg
¼ cup sugar
5 tablespoons unsalted butter, chilled and cubed
1 egg
¾ cup milk
12 ounces strawberries
5 tablespoons sugar
2 tablespoons Grand Marnier
1½ cups heavy cream

Method:

1. Preheat oven to 450 degrees.

2. Sift together the flour, baking powder, salt, nutmeg, and ¼ cup sugar into a bowl. Drop in the butter pieces, and quickly rub to a crumb texture. Beat the egg into the milk, and pour onto the dry mixture. Mix until a smooth dough is formed.

3. On a lightly floured worktable, roll out the dough until it is ½-inch thick. Cut out 6 2-inch rounds of dough with a biscuit cutter and 18 3-inch-long diamonds. Place cut-out dough on a lightly buttered or a nonstick baking pan. Bake for 20 minutes.

4. Reserve six strawberries for decoration. Slice the remaining strawberries, and sprinkle with 2 tablespoons of sugar and 1 tablespoon of Grand Marnier.

5. In a chilled bowl, beat the heavy cream with the remaining sugar and Grand Marnier just until stiff peaks form.

6. Place a round of pastry on each of 6 dessert plates. Cover the pastry with the sliced strawberries. Pipe out a large rosette of whipped cream through a pastry bag and a star tube. Garnish the whipped cream with three diamond pastries and a reserved strawberry.

Photograph on page 240

Pastries with Bavarian Cream and Cognac

(Serves 12 to 14)

Ingredients:
2 cups unbleached, all-purpose flour
1 egg, lightly beaten
¼ cup cold water
2 tablespoons granulated sugar
1 teaspoon pure vanilla extract
3 cups vegetable oil
4 cups whole milk
1 cup granulated sugar
½ cup cornstarch
2 eggs
2 egg yolks
2 teaspoons pure vanilla extract
2 cups heavy cream
⅓ cup brown sugar
1 teaspoon pure vanilla extract
2 tablespoons Cognac
confectioners sugar and cinnamon
1 pint strawberries, cleaned with their stems left on
a few mint sprigs

Method:

1. In a bowl, add the flour, egg, water, 2 tablespoons granulated sugar, and 1 teaspoon vanilla extract. Knead for a few minutes until a smooth, elastic, somewhat sticky dough is formed. Add more water if necessary. On a floured surface, roll out dough to approximately ⅛-inch in thickness or until the surface of the worktable can be seen through the dough. Cut into 1- by 3-inch rectangular strips. Deep-fry in 3 cups of preheated 375-degree oil until golden brown. Drain the pastries on paper towels.

2. In a saucepan, bring the milk and ½ cup of granulated sugar to a boil. In the meantime, in a bowl, mix the cornstarch, the remaining ½ cup of granulated sugar, eggs, and egg yolks until they are thoroughly blended and free of all lumps from the cornstarch. Temper the egg mixture by adding approximately ⅓ cup hot milk to the egg mixture. Now pour the egg mixture into the saucepan with the boiling milk. Stir until the mixture comes to a boil. Remove from heat, add 2 teaspoons of vanilla extract, and store the custard in a covered bowl in the refrigerator until chilled.

(Recipe continued on next page.)

5. Unmold the mousse onto a serving platter by placing the outside of the cake pan in a warm bath for approximately 30 seconds. Place the serving platter on top of the mousse, and flip the cake pan over so that the mousse slides onto the platter. With a spatula, smooth out the top and sides of the mousse. Clean the platter with a warm, wet towel, then refrigerate to firm before decorating.

6. Using a pastry bag and star tube, pipe out the decorating cream along the sides and top of the mousse.

7. Roll out red colored almond paste between 2 sheets of wax paper. Cut out small hearts with a heart shaped hors d'oeuvre cutter. Decorate the border of the mousse with hearts, and the center of the mousse with a red rose (see illustration).

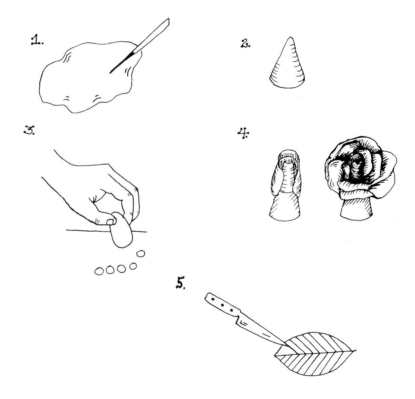

(To make red roses)

Method: 1. With a toothpick, add a small touch of red food coloring to some almond paste. Mix until the desired color is obtained. It is best not to mix completely. Gradations of color make the roses look more realistic.

(Recipe continued on next page.)

2. Form a small 1-inch cone and place it upside down on a worktable.

3. Form ½-inch balls, then pinch them between index finger and thumb to form petals. Work with a dampened cloth to prevent fingers from sticking to almond paste.

4. Curl the first few petals around the top of the cone. Work the remaining petals down, out, and around until the rose is formed.

5. To make green leaves, follow method 1 using green food coloring. Pinch to shape into leaves, place on a worktable, and score with a paring knife to make leaf veins.

Photograph on page 207

Sunday's Dessert

(Serves 6)

Ingredients: 2 cups fresh cranberries
¼ cup sugar
1 cup water
plain 2% yogurt
6 slices kiwi fruit
12 slices strawberry
6 dried apricots, soaked in ½ cup apple juice overnight
6 honeydew melon balls or 6 bing cherries
6 sprigs fresh peppermint
cinnamon

Method:

1. In a saucepan, add the cranberries, sugar, and water. Stir, and cook over high heat until the water has been completely reduced. Set aside and let cool.

2. Place a small scoop of yogurt and a small scoop of the cranberry sauce on one side of 6 champagne glasses. Place a slice of kiwi fruit, 2 slices of strawberry, and an apricot on the other side. Place a melon ball in the center. Garnish with a sprig of fresh peppermint, and sprinkle the yogurt with a little cinnamon.

3. Cover glasses with plastic wrap, and refrigerate until serving time.

Photograph on page 202

Babas Au Rhum

yeast cake with raisins soaked in a hot rum sauce

(Makes 1½ dozen cakes)

Ingredients: 1 package dry yeast
¼ cup warm water
2 cups unbleached, all-purpose flour
¼ cup sugar
⅛ teaspoon salt
4 eggs
1 cup soft butter
1 cup raisins

Method:

1. Sprinkle the dry yeast over the warm water. Let it stand for 15 to 20 minutes.

2. Add ½ cup flour, the sugar, and the salt.

3. Beat the eggs in one at a time, and gradually add the remaining flour with the soft butter. Mix well until the mixture is smooth.

4. Place the dough in a bowl, cover with plastic wrap or a wet towel, and place in a warm area for approximately 30 minutes until the dough is double in bulk.

5. Stir the dough down, add the raisins, and distribute into muffin tins one-half full. Let the batter rise until it reaches the top of the mold.

6. Bake in a preheated 350 degree oven for approximately 15 to 20 minutes. Babas Au Rhum cakes can be made ahead of time and frozen at this stage. Prepare Hot Rum Sauce before serving (see next recipe).

Photograph on page 180

Photographs

Carrot and Pea Hors D'Oeuvres (page 15)

Cinderella Salad (page 40) with Magic Wands (page 106)

Banana Squash Purée with Mixed Vegetables (page 91)

Belgium Endive and Salmon Salad Canapés (page 14)

Holiday Fruit Platter (page 126)

Pasta and Vegetable Salad (page 18)

Eggs Albert (page 116)

Duck Consommé with Red Peppercorns and Spinach (page 20)

Chicken Salad Erika (page 21)

Twelve Seasons Lobster Tails (page 58)

Broiled Breast of Chicken Teriyaki (page 69), Coriander Sweet Potatoes (page 95),
Green Beans with Red Pepper and Honey-Roasted Pecans (page 93)

Phoenician Salmon Salad (page 36)

Baked Apples (page 125)

Spinach, Beets, and Belgium Endive Salad (page 32)

Tomato-Basil Noodles with Pistachio Nuts and Garlic (page 81)

Peach-Almond Granola (page 85)

Purée of Fresh Pea Soup (page 27)

Mrs. Jay's Wedding Cake (page 156)

Tenderloin of Venison with Cognac Sauce and Walnuts (page 70)

Cleopatra's Platter (page 82)

Chilled Strawberry Soup (page 28)

Roast Rack of Lamb Gregory (page 75) with Asparagus (page 92) and Red Potatoes (page 88)

Ruth's Fruit (page 121)

Special Cookie (page 139)

Orange Freeze (page 11)

Mixed Grilled Vegetables with Fresh Water Chestnuts (page 110)

Seafood Bisque (page 34)

Black Bean Chile (page 104)

Poppy's Rice Plate (page 102)

Orange Roughy Delmont (page 47)

Mama Es' Noodle Pudding (page 107)

Cream Puffs over Hot Fudge Sauce (page 143)

Snake Bread (page 108)

Thanksgiving Cake (page 154)

Sunday's Dessert (page 151)

Chicken Klotz-Reilly (page 76)

Zucchini and Green Bean Canapés (page 7)

Nectarines with Prunes (page 127)

Green Onion and Mushroom Quesadilla with Southwest Salsa (page 118)

Saturday Night's Chocolate Soufflé (page 137)

White Chocolate- Graham Cracker Clusters (page 135)

A Chocolate Mousse for Saint Valentine's Day (page 148)

Jennifer's Snow Ball Hors D'Oeuvres (page 13)

Shrimp Fantasia (page 56)

Sebastian Sandwich (page 71) with Marinated Cauliflower, Carrot, and Rutabaga Salad (page 31)

Sunburst Salad (page 41)

— 214 —

Scrambled Eggs with Chile Peppers and Cheese (page 120)

Vegetables O'Keefe (page 84)

Pryce Salad (page 25)

Broccoli and Mushroom Parmesan with Red and Yellow Peppers (page 89)

Chicken and Celery Bisteeya (page 64) with Cherry Tomato and Bean Salad (page 19)

Gingered Chicken Breast Salad (page 29)

Celery, Peas, and Smokehouse Almonds (page 101)

Sherry-Ginger Dressing, Green Cucumber Salsa
Spinach Dressing, Roquefort Cheese Dressing, Raspberry-Walnut Dressing
Soy and Sesame Seed Dressing (pages 42-44)

Carrots and Broccoli with Soy and Sesame Seed Dressing (page 105)

Super Chocolate Chip Cookies (page 133)

Baklava (page 140)

Rossen Salad (page 35)

Kiwi Fruit, Mangoes, and Berries (page 117)

Vegetable-Bean Soup (page 37) with a Whole Wheat Roll, Fresh Fruit and Butter (page 100)

Veal Medallions with Red Peppercorns, Fresh Thyme, and Truffles (page 73)

Sliced Fruit (page 117)

Sliced Fruit (page 117)

Mussels with Saffron Potatoes (page 48)

Ricky Hors D'Oeuvres (page 12)

Almond-Dusted Swordfish (page 49)

Nancy's Lemon Bars (page 145)

Barbecued Pork Tenderloin (page 63) with Orange Slaw Salad (page 38)

Peach Brandy Mousse (page 146)

C.D.'s Dessert (page 158)

Quail and Kumquat Tagine with Fresh Chives (page 68)

The number in the first column indicates the page on which the recipe appears.
The number in the second column indicates the page on which the photograph appears.

INDEX

The number in the first column indicates the page on which the recipe appears.
The number in the second column indicates the page on which the photograph appears.